PRAISE FOR SAM HEAPS

Calling this book "brave" is an understatement. This is a dizzying, heartbreaking punch-to-the-gut masterwork. Heaps rides through their past like Kali, forging something that is equal parts beautiful and terrifying.

— JULIET ESCORIA, AUTHOR OF *BLACK CLOUD* AND
JULIET THE MANIAC

Roman á clef, erotic memoir, and scathing breakup letter, *Proximity* pulses with pain and desire, requires total abandonment, and demands that we take pleasure in the way it wounds us. I felt drunk on its power.

— SARAH GERARD, AUTHOR OF *SUNSHINE STATE*
AND *TRUE LOVE*

Proximity, as a noun, is the singular most important aspect of how to love another person. How close can you be to a person, and how close they can be to you, defines an entire relationship—the distance therein an experience of euphoria or abject fright. Heaps' essay collection will grip you, from one end to the other of this experience. Prepare to be ravaged.

— ELLE NASH, AUTHOR OF *GAG REFLEX* AND
ANIMALS EAT EACH OTHER

GW00569077

Equally invested in noticing and being noticed, Heaps's memoir achieves a statelieness that narratives about sexual reckonings rarely obtain. Ostensively a narrative of desire (and awkwardly, gutturally, blissfully, there is *much* of that), what emerges from their story is not a diary of titillation, but a beautiful and elegiac love story. It is an autopsy all the same—and a startling one.

— J. HOWARD ROSIER, BOARD MEMBER,
NATIONAL BOOK CRITICS CIRCLE

Proximity is a fearless debut—a formally adventurous book that stunned me with pleasure. Shrewd and wrenching, sacred and profane, *Proximity* takes an unsentimental look at sex and gender, power and poverty. Heaps may have starved themselves— physically and psychically—but in this book they sing the flesh back onto their bones.

— SARA LEVINE, AUTHOR OF *TREASURE ISLAND!!!*
AND *SHORT DARK ORACLES*

The ancient Greeks regarded eros as disruptive and often ruinous; a form of delirium that alights upon our lives and changes us utterly, not always for the better. In this modern age, a whole lot of us act (and write) as if there's an eventual order, even romance of the halcyon variety, to the whole endeavor. But not Sam Heaps, who possesses the unnerving and exceptional ability to render this sort of wanting as the affliction that it really is, however much pleasure might come with it.

In *Proximity*, desire is hot-blooded and alive in all its delirious, wounding, ecstatic manifestations.

— ALINA PLESKOVA, AUTHOR OF *TOSKA* AND CO-
EDITOR OF *BEDFELLOWS*

Proximity is haunting, stylish, and bold—a beautiful, aching litany of want. Full of heat and relentless lust, bald vulnerability, and unapologetic darkness, this book skillfully excavates desire, turns it inside out, touches every part of it. Heaps is a ferocious talent, and this is a heart-shattering debut.

— KIMBERLY KING PARSONS, AUTHOR OF *BLACK LIGHT*

"Fiercely intelligent and intense, *Proximity* asks readers to enter the dark heart of desire. It's the rare kind of complex, immersive work that reminds you that to fall in love is to find both heaven and hell."

— LINDSAY LERMAN, AUTHOR OF *WHAT ARE YOU*

"Sam Heaps writes like a banshee with their hair on fire, like a force of nature. The many desires at the lusty heart of their exhilarating debut remind us of all that is lost and all that is gained when we give ourselves over— even for just a few minutes—to another human being. It revels in and celebrates its wide-eyed openness to every physical sensation. There's freedom here, and joy. It's beautiful. *Proximity* reads to me like an immediate classic of erotic literature that is also so much more than that."

— ANDREW ERVIN, AUTHOR OF *BURNING DOWN GEORGE ORWELL'S HOUSE*

PROXIMITY

SAM HEAPS

CL◢SH

The idea of a person's being a thing is a logical contradiction. Yet what is impossible in logic becomes true in life, and the contradiction lodged within the soul tears it to shreds.

— *THE POEM OF FORCE*, SIMONE WEIL

PROXIMITY

I

A.

On a run I approach and you turn too suddenly. Your mask. Like a nightmare.

Your wife the same afternoon. Her contented happy gait. Her Mary Janes and the baby strapped to her chest. The wide berth I afford her. The way I watch her as she walks.

If only I could be her.

XCIV

As soon as you are in the apartment just coiled against each other you hold my feet, massaging. I run my hands along your back over and over drinking up the skin around a raised tattoo — your face buried in me from behind you run your tongue up from my clit and around the rim of my ass. The intimacy is enormous, as if we are well known lovers when we have never met before. When, we have never spoken before an hour earlier. We are starving though and it seems worth almost anything. The feeling of flesh. Hands inside my mouth, holding me back, pushing me down. Something that I do not control.

The neighbors across the alley have a balcony on which they sun. Throughout the quarantine their windows face mine and I watch their daily lives. The man works in the kitchen, the woman in the bedroom. She has wide hips that he sometimes grips with affection as she passes him. Together they eat pasta for lunch — I can smell the boiling starches. Herbs and spices. At night smoking weed. The woman drinks only white wine. They laugh together with easy frequency. Laugh loud. The blinds are never lowered as if they are performing for me so I might know how much I am lacking. The woman sometimes will toe the fourth wall, meeting my blue eyes with hers. Almost the same shade.

This night is the only time I break the rules for several long months. Fifty, sixty days.

I hope the reader will forgive me these two hours of weakness. But, if the reader cannot, let it be known now this book is not only about things that should be forgiven.

I have a dream about you A. You tie me up the way you sometimes bind your wife but so loose my limbs and skin have to grow, inflate, to reach the intricate restraints. I can see you over my shoulder stroking yourself, but you will not give me what I want as I continue to thicken. I tell you I don't like this game. Vulnerable like this and I am not as pretty as she in the shape. So hungry. Growing bigger still but with emptiness. You open an incision with a sharpened fingernail from your wrist to the inside of your elbow. A dirty fingernail. In a photo your wife has dirt beneath her nails. Unclean. You open the wound with her stained fingers which sprout from your body. Widening the wound so I am allowed to lap up the blood with my kitten tongue while you grip at your cock.

And I wake naked and alone in the empty bed, a used condom next to the pillow.

I cum. I cry.

I

Maybe eight here. Somewhere between eight and ten. Probably this goes on for several years. My mother is wise enough not to let me sleep at your house. Your uncle believes he is a certain type of man when he is another, answering the door in sheer Mormon garments so I can see the outline of his genitals.

There is a joke my father makes about molestation, to me, when I am a child. I cannot remember it in full. Why it was supposed to be funny. The extent to which I understood.

You ask me to fuck you on our apartment's small playground. I am on a swing.

You see me and maybe you are angry. You ask me to fuck you. I say, I don't know what that means. You laugh at me. I don't know fuck, a tall boy in my grade using it once looking at a pairing of grasshoppers. I don't even know sex. I learn the word rape in a book before I have been given "the talk." When I learn it, no more than nine, reading a series about World War II. A Nazi officer corners a German woman in her kitchen and she asks, *are you going to rape me?*

To my mother. What does it mean?

I don't know what you mean when you ask to fuck me or how sincere you are in your intent. You are, maybe three years older and just as precocious in your early puberty. Tall and athletic. Absolutely incomprehensibly wild. Where I feel nothing, you feel everything.

As a punishment for an unknown crime your uncle shaves your thick brown hair. In a story I compare it to the bark of a felled redwood. Wavy. Your nose is dusted with freckles and they are illuminated by the buzzcut. You are bullied by other children in the apartment complex as you are so strange and you cry too much but I am popular enough to do whatever I want and I like you and I always let you play with me, war games mostly. We are both excellent climbers and we sit in our high perches and spy for approaching armies. We build a little haven on a hill, hanging a swing between two trees with a foot long sheet of plywood your aunt helps us drill holes in and that we feed thick plastic-covered electrical cords through. Your aunt is a very gentle woman. The line between gentle and broken I question here, but regardless I never see her unkind to you. Long red hair with flyaways, she is so thin. She choreographs a dance for church and it is you and me and we are virtues I believe. Feminine virtues like faith or purity.

There are different games too where you are the wife and I am the husband. I think I remember you liked to feel pretty and girlish in a way that you weren't often allowed and in a way that was forced upon me. A way I hated. I push you on the swing. Maybe we kiss. Yes we are children, but can we not be lovesick too?

XLVIII

The women are always too good for me. You have everything planned.

My tongue in your mouth at the party, trying to lead you into bed. You like the folk band downstairs but when you see the chaos in my room — the paintings, the dirty dishes, the piles of dresses where there should be sheets — you shake your head at the threshold. *I'm not sleeping in there.*

White wine and a stovetop. My hair pinned back in suspenders to impress upon you I am as queer as I have promised. Waking in your bed to see you already working on your laptop in the corner even though the morning has barely begun.

Walking along Broad Street sucking on a lollipop — convinced I can win you on charm. Bragging to hide my terror. You wanted to play the game though and either I cannot keep up or I cannot follow the rules. I tell myself I hate the rules. Your elliptical your house your double major. You see the order now upended. Walking down empty streets do you recognize your false idol?

Or, sitting in your home, have you created more lies to bow down to.

A., has your wife?

LXVI

You say you love my discipline. I say come with me to Nagarkot. Your English is bad but my Spanish is worse. Pushing. On the balcony the morning after the mountain in thick clouds so we might be alone — just spiders spinning in their webs — our hands and more clouds settling on our shoulders. Smoking cigarettes together while I read Eugenides over tea. On the hike back down you cannot keep up. I am too strong for you sieving back into the world of man. I am embarrassed you have proven to be so delicate.

XLV

You are a "funny man," so this is the one where I learn to cum
from joy. You are standing next to the bed after we are finished
and I am smiling looking up at you. We are always talking,
constant banter — and again, we begin. I comment on poor
Mayor Pete and you do an impression in the nude. I laugh, rise,
stand at your shoulder in the mirror. I touch myself. I whisper in
your ear. Now Warren. You mock the senator, unkindly. She is
my favorite candidate and you know it, so your imitation is a
cruel one. Something about the humiliation of the jabs, the pleasure of your hot flesh in my hand, the sensation of being so very
alive.

I cum.

The memory sweet and self-sustaining. Pausing here to
remember.

But we are a binary and there is the bathtub as well.

Sitting on the floor watching television I am stroking your head on
my lap when the world shifts. I am not so sure I know where I am.

I do not want you to see me cry we have been fighting all day and
I do not know what you will do if you see me break down so I
walk to the bathroom. The bathroom is too big. I do not know how
to stand I try to sit. I sit in front of the door. *Sam? You need to let
me in. Sam?* I let you open the door and I am trembling and I have
the need to bleed deep it will feel better and you are too close now
here in the space and so I climb into the tub and the tub is better
but also terrible and so big and I cower in a corner. Don't touch
me. You don't. I hold my arms against my chest and at first maybe
I am not even weeping but rocking and I cannot breathe. Then
weeping. Weeping hysterically. I am so scared I am so scared.

How many scenes of this manner to include? There are plenty
of these to come. Once you, reader, understand their shape you
are welcome to skip ahead to more salacious bits.

I think is only fair to include this one though because I am not
always kind. And, look here how much kindness is offered to
me. Illustrating this point of contrast.

You sit on your knees in the bathroom without touching for an
hour. After I give permission you step inside the tub and sit near
me, still, not touching. We watch cartoons like this until I have
stopped shaking enough to let you hold me. I lie against you in
the tub until the early morning and then you take me to bed and
allow me to cling to you still there.

Only a few hours later. This morning we have decided will be
your last morning as my lover. After we fuck it is your turn
to cry.

This is how it is with us. All ups. All downs. White. Black. We
are both so lonely and angry and desperate — so willing to
throw everything away for anything. Perhaps we resent one
another this state mirrored.

You tell me when we were young, the first time, that our love affair was grand. But I have forgotten you existed. I haven't. But also, I must have. Who else is running through my life without my having any memory of them? In anticipation of this silly little project, or maybe to try to make some of sense of the passing time, I cover my walls with brown paper and begin an inventory.

Here it becomes tricky though. Do I include someone I loved but did not fuck? Do I include fucks whose names I don't remember? Do I include emotional affairs and flirtations and young crushes? _____ sitting on hot black asphalt under the Idaho stars. I never again show this moment of passion. There are many missing bodies and moments. I ultimately decide to include who I am compelled to include and hope that intuition itself will create a system of classification through which to sort a life.

You say, when we're fifty, if we're both single, let's move into a house together. *I'll get fat. You'll get too thin.* I say I want sherry. Casks.

I don't remember it being volatile when we were young, but this second time everything is hyper-pigmentation of mood. We're so busy fucking we forget to eat. We're so busy fighting we have to fight while we fuck. Or talking. We play in bed and have full conversations while you are inside of me. Sometimes you speak to me in Russian, dipping your face back between my thighs between words. I wish I knew the words. They were the right kind of angry to be inherently sensual. Our conversations are arguments. We disagree even on the things we agree on. Every time I call you grudgingly say you will stay, maybe just an hour, still angry from the last time. Every time you crawl out of my bed four days later haggard and I am bruised like a peach and red-eyed, empty whiskey bottles in the kitchen. When did we sleep? But when would there have been the hours for it. Too much to do.

The first time must not help though. You're in the city after years abroad. At first I cannot place your name to a face, but we take a long walk and enjoy one another's company so much that I decide to bring you back to my place, forgetting the brown paper. Quite forgetting that in my inventory of cocks and cunts your name did not make the list. You, for whatever reason, are not part of this matrix that is creating itself in front of my eyes.

What I remember of the first time? — Small pieces. But many overlapped with other men around your age, or shape, who I was dating at the same time. Some older. A woman here too, and a couple. A few have their chapters coming. I did not believe any of you particularly cared for me. I could not fathom it might have hurt you to know I was with someone else. I always imagined, but maybe this is disguised selfishness, that you would have been happy not to tolerate me so often. I see one of your contemporaries in the grocery store this week. His eyes wide with shock, the oranges behind him illuminating the expanding whites — so I must have made an impression. And yet, he also did not make the list. Since this will be his last appearance, he was a boy scout.

I ask, why did we end? *You were living with your professor?* A question. Oh yes, I remember now, I was.

I remember playing video games after class with your roommate. I love the slink of Centipede. I remember you walking me home. I remember you cooking with eggplant and I remember you buying me cases of beer on hot summer nights. The way you stand on crowded subway platforms.

I remember after breaking a condom you rolling into a ball on the bed. *I can't be a father I can't be a father.* The disgust I felt for you without a hint of sympathy. I myself had already experienced this moment so many times I was intolerant of your naivety. After we have already seen what sympathies you are later able to offer me. I think you paid for the morning after pill but I'm almost sure I went to buy it myself — forced to take care of my own needs in a way I truly bristle at.

I remember just as vividly a night where we ordered two pizzas and watched *The Sheltering Sky* and I ate my entire pie but you saved half of yours. I asked you why and you told me it is for later, a concept I have no ability to grasp. What is later? You have the pizza just for the now. There's no way to know where it might run off to in an hour or who you might be. Whether you will be around to eat it at all.

I remember now there were so many men around this time, because in part, I was hungry.

I remember changing into stilettos, smoking, leaning against the pillars of City Hall. I remember you watching.

This second time you request — after good months of brunch and lovemaking and care, with caveats and compromises, careful not to spook me — monogamy. You say you love me, which I do not believe. I ultimately consent but just twelve hours later, maybe even eight, I have another man in my bed. I call you as he's walking out the door to request my punishment.

Tell me. Tell me you cannot love a worm. Tell me you cannot love a mere receptacle for cum, a slithering dirty whore. Tell me.

Why with you A.? How did you convince me I could be of value? I did not even put up a fight.

And do you care this too is why he leaves me A.? Pushes so hard for promises of faithfulness that he knows I cannot provide?

Seeing you on the street with the baby a few months after the first time you leave me. The last time I saw the child he was still just a thickness in your wife's waist. My want for you is so strong that meeting I can almost sense it pooling around us on the sidewalk, sticking us to where we stand. At night he tells me, *I don't want to be hurt like A.'s wife. I see you still love him.* And I swear it is not true. But, you A., dearest reader. You see how I am lying. And this is when I am asked to promise fidelity.

It feels so cruel to say if you read this. Any of you. There is a moment when sex is urgent and there are no condoms and I send you (any you) across the street to buy one from the corner store. The playful intimacy of returning with two or three, depending on how ambitious you are, how poor you are, single Magnums.

You, any you, return and we laugh. *Don't be disappointed.* And it seems like a moment that should only happen once. That should just be shared with one person. And each time is a blurring of every time it has happened before and the loneliness of it, to be the only witness. To be the only one of a supposedly intimate pair to know the joke is not special at all.

The last time I see you is after we are done and we are friendly. I ask if you will watch television with me. I ask you to take the painting, I don't want it looking at me anymore. But still, it is across from me now, hanging on my bedroom wall as I write this. Such a funny painting so that no one who fucks me even asks. It is clear. I am hysterical. Very funny. You are a funny man and I a funny woman and it is a funny painting.

I spend every holiday of this year alone. From Christmas to Christmas. This is the life I have built. So, Thanksgiving is no exception. It is after I have hurt you most brutally and you tell me you cannot love me. Will not come back. And I paint feverishly all day. I do nothing but paint and think of you.

You always tell me, *the sex is not that important, please stop making it about the sex.* You pity me, you say, I hope at least partly in jest, if this sex matters so much to you.

Maybe it always matters this much to me. It is the essential piece. It is all I am sure I can offer.

This painting is my favorite painting of mine other than one I have done of you A. Are you reading this A.? Recently. Standing in the Impressionist galleries at the Philadelphia Museum of Art while you hold your child. But I like this one too. Five feet by three. Descending from heaven with the halo of a medieval saint you outstretch your arms in my apartment. Nude. Glowing. You are the only thing in the painting to have clear features. Everything else is muted and washed. I am barely there at all. An angry red blur in the corner of the canvas. Very funny. It is a little bit of a joke, just for me.

As we watch television we settle into our old shape. You rest your head in my lap and I stroke back your hair. The familiar smell of your cologne and the musty scalp beneath. When I attempt to instigate more you say it is time for you to go. I am petty and without words. Juvenile I pout at your rejection. I turn away from you. You leave without the painting. Without saying goodbye. Without locking the door behind you. That's all.

A.

Sometimes when I fantasize about fucking women I feel I must invent a man to watch and condone before I can finish.

This book then is maybe not as pompous as an attempt to give my life narrative, but instead merely an attempt to have my life seen — to make myself visible to you A., so clearly defined, manifested publicly. A., Domain of Male, Phylum of Author, Order of Husband, Genus of Father. Species of Relentlessly Adored. Will you look at me so that I have permission, purpose, to continue on?

Where are the stories of the other woman? Where do they go after the tawdry affair is completed? When the man is returned to his good woman and all is right in the world — when there is no one to look at the needy home-wrecking wretches anymore — where do they go? I would be so grateful if they disappeared, as we assume they must. Their stories must end once the man will no longer look at them — invisible and insubstant interchangeable. But, I am not gone. I am still bathing myself and feeding myself and shitting and grieving and taking long mournful walks. I am discarded and there is no container to suit

the kind of waste I have become. But still, I filter through the air.
I catch in trees, groaning.

Sometimes I am lucky enough not to feel heartbreak. Or... rage.
But then, opening a book, a gift, to find again your handwriting
A. You say, I love your work. You say, I love your view on the
world. But mostly, this is what you say without fabrication. You
say, mostly — *I just love you.*

What would be a nobler hurt than these? These puny pleas.

When you hold her every night I wonder if you say to her, *this
has made our marriage stronger.* I wonder if you look at each
other with new assured commitment. *If we can get through this*
— and the baby may cry interrupting. I wonder how soon after
you come home does she let you fuck her. Maybe she does not
even want to wait, so happy to have you back. I wonder if you
cry holding her after. I think of you sitting with the child,
marveling at the way he is like both of you together. I see a
photo of the boy grown. Her delicate wrists supporting your son
while you coo and awe. You say you listen to her sing to him.
She is not only loved by you, close to you — but observed in your
days and in your life. Corporeal.

I swear I am not gone though. I am merely unobserved and
decaying and mad.

How to swallow without the gaze, the grace, to bless the throat
— to tell it, you are deserving. I allow for your sustenance.

XXVII

After you rape me you tell people how disappointing I am in bed. Like a limp fish.

My manager at the store. Late nights. Organizing and reorganizing the shelves.

Now you write the news.

LXII

A canyon. A sunset. A blanket on the back of your trunk.

Long blonde dreads and a peace sign necklace.

Don't you know, it wouldn't have happened if you didn't deserve it. We are all being punished for sins we committed in a past life. Leaning in for a kiss.

LXXIX

We meet at a party on July Fourth. Your older brother is wearing my dress — red white and blue with polka dots and puffy sleeves — and I am wearing your brother's T-Shirt and gym shorts and we are making out on a picnic blanket. His head in my lap and I am kissing him while the fireworks erupt overhead. A hat trick, I think, is what days like these are called.

You are not the only one who tries to get me home that night, but you are the most persistent and so the one who is ultimately successful. I lie on the futon while you go out to get condoms and when you return my door is locked. You say you want me so much though you kick it in.

You are sheltered and giddy. You like your friends and psychedelics and disc golf. You come over to my bedroom and we chatter. Fuck. Chatter. Bicker.

I donate clothing to your alter-ego. Small floral dresses and white lace. I like to see how pretty she is in the things I have chosen. She is submissive and groomed and wants to please me but I am disappointed by the size of the cock she wants me to fuck her with. Can't she take any more? Looking down at the strap-on along my hips and the small plastic phallus protruding. This isn't me. I would have so much more to offer her.

I spend Christmas with you and your family one year. They have a farm with chickens and the land is beautiful. Your two older brothers, three incredibly different species of men, and you the clear baby, stay up with us drinking and playing games.

Your mother has gifts for me when I arrive. She has wrapped things from around the house so I will have something to open and I pine for her still. A package of pasta. An old book. AAA batteries. And I'm not sure if I'm supposed to but I keep the gifts, still. You are like her. Visiting me later in Montana and you teach me how to hold my dog. That if I am not afraid of her rejection she will come to me and let me put my arm around her. You promise you and your partner will look after her.

We have sex in your mother's house, the last time, and it is very sweet. And you ask me after. *Did we just make love?*

IX

You lose your virginity to a man in his twenties the weekend my grandmother buys me my harp. I do not know when the aid was bestowed or to what degree. My grandmother paid for my dance classes. She bought me my good brown leather shoes. She insisted when she visited, that we eat, and well. She would hold my mother — who she loved it seemed more than her own son — to her large breasts while my mother wept. *Oh honey. It gets better.*

I cannot complain about money and also have a harp.

But the apartment it was in, the frame, was monstrous in its filthiness. Its despair. It smelled of cigarette smoke and there was graffiti on the walls outside. Poverty in Idaho had spoiled us. There we could run. In Maryland, near Baltimore, it is gunshots and the barbed wire fence around the McDonalds and somehow no light made it through the windows. Every memory I have of the place is dark. No electricity the first day of school combing back my hair in a dark mirror.

And in that hell I have a harp.

I am obsessed with you. You move to the school halfway through
Freshman year and are a fellow Alto 2 in choir. Sometimes we
sing the tenor part if they are short on boys, and it is a joyful
rebellion to me. I am, in an off way, popular in this school. I am
also new. Forced into a remedial English class because the
administrators imagine I cannot be used to academic rigor. I do
not resist but I climb my way back up the ladder each subsequent year. I will do a book report on *War and Peace* for one
such low-level course. I still remember carefully reading the
book, post-its every two pages. A dearness I still feel for Pierre. I
will also show up to class so drug addled I will be unable to
complete a wordsearch. But this depravity also brings its own
social clout and initially you need me. And I am engorged
with you.

You're going to be a model, it is your driving force. So confident
and pure with single- minded intent. You are maybe the most
beautiful person I have ever been in the presence of. Now you
wear your hair natural, I know because I was recently startled to
see you look at me from a clothing advertisement. Not look.
Then, you straightened it I think, maybe a little bleached strand
of faded green. Perfectly Scene. In the mornings in safety
pinned leather jackets you would re-pierce your snake eyes,
removing them every night when you went home. While I
watched. And _____ next to you watched me watch you.

When you begin to move beyond me, older prettier boys and
girls at richer schools, or in their twenties in bands, bringing
vodka in water bottles to health class, you try to bring me along.
We smoke menthol cigarettes along the water behind the mall.
You shoplift at Forever 21 and I cover for you but am too afraid
to do it myself. We walk. You tell me about your life, music,
anything. You try to dress me. I wear nothing but wide jeans
and black hoodies. Men's T- shirts. You say, *you could look so
pretty if you tried*. But I don't believe you. I try once though to
impress you. A blue summer dress I wear over a white T-shirt

and tight bell bottoms. You offer encouragement, approval, while I watch you fix the thick lines over your eyes.

I remember I loved your smell, but I cannot remember what it was comprised of. You told me you liked mine too, but it was cigarette smoke from the apartment and laundry detergent. Soap. I have always scoured myself raw.

Changing next to you in gym. Too stupid not to look. When you point out my Oscar the Grouch bra from Walmart, clearly wearing through.

You will post a comment on my blog years later. *I remember you, funny and tough in your neon green bra.* Knowing you were looking at me too, and that you saw me. I am funny. I am tough.

You are firm but kind in your rebuff and I am clear in my intent, when I ask, lurch forward. *I don't go that way Sam.* When you will not let me kiss you, I call you a slur. I don't even know how I knew the slur or how I could associate it with you. You point out I've chosen the wrong word, and also I am lucky you don't slap me. Later you offer to hold my hair back if I need to vomit.

I know the person who does this is me. As I already told you, this book is not written so that I, any of us, may be granted forgiveness. It is an archive for its own sake. There is no atonement I offer. Not to you A., not to myself.

The weekend you lose your virginity is the first time I touch the harp and hold it between my thighs and listen to each string as I tune it obsessively throughout the day. Trying to find the perfect pitch. Nothing but glissandos for hours. And leaning it back onto my shoulder, rocking with it.

You tell me after your first time, *he said he loved me.* I stiffen — but you are so smart. *I know what he meant was this feels so good* *and he doesn't really **love** me*. Infinitely wise. Were I to learn this lesson from you. You make a motion, continue to describe the acts as they occurred and I am rapt. You imply we were both making love that weekend. I to my instrument. You, she, to.

This week, gripping the instrument tight between my thighs as I unthread a broken F string. Chords that no matter how they're tuned sound so, so lonely.

VI

Your death is like sitting down where there is no chair. I did not
know you well but I knew you were the best of us, an absolutely
true statement. Practicing kissing for the director. She says,
come on _____, don't you think she's pretty?

I am fourteen. You're a senior. I have never kissed anyone like
this before. Both my legs over one of your thighs. Your big hands
around my cheeks. In every scene the director puts us in the
center of the stage. Don't fake it. And so, we kiss. Grope. But
never anything more than I agree to and never off of the stage.
You never tease me like many of the other boys do but always
behave with a code of honor, a chivalry. You tell your friends
you feel bad for me, that I am so shy.

Your greatest fear was nothing to do with mortality, or physical
suffering, but instead failure. That fear seemed so wise and
incomprehensibly deep. I feared pain. Nothing greater.
Arriving at rehearsal with your new tattoo too sore to lift me.

After your death I find an old DVD of the play and there is a
scene where you pull me away from a fight by holding me from

behind, lifting me, setting me down on the other side of the stage. And I remember the kick of arousal that close to your body. I remember you infinitely soft-spoken. I remember being abashed by your easy popularity.

Beloved.

VII

Fourteen still. Maybe we have been flirting over the internet. In fact, I am sure we have. I am sure I tell you I want you, because I do. But when you put your hand on the wall behind me and move to kiss me. I am suddenly afraid. The confines of the arm and the torso.

You are a successful rapper now. Whenever you are in my city on tours you reach out. I always listen to your music and tell myself I will go, and, I never go.

A.

You take notes once when you are with me. *Things I love about Sam*, but you will not show it to me. It must not have been a very long list. You say, *I have no photos of you*, lamenting, but you do not rectify the issue. You say you will not write of me and expect gratitude.

A story you write about your wife. Her little toes. Her vibrating butt plug. Your enormous desire for her and only her. Multiplying, copulating with itself and shitting out more want. More.

XXIII

Addicts. Handcuffed to your bed frame two nights after begging you to kill me on your floor. Vomiting on your roommate's shoes. And you understand you say but you won't do it. Fucking me so raw I am cut open inside and I bleed and the wound heals sour because we do not stop fucking, I do not want you to stop fucking me — swollen, so tight almost closed until you tell me I have to go to the doctor. *We've taken this too far.* You take a photo of me drinking malt liquor and writing on your desktop and it is a favorite. My long black hair done in curls and my arms thin.

Are these nothing more than documentation? To give you what you no longer want A.?

Or, to preoccupy myself with revisitations.

LXVIII

My last week in Hanoi we spend a night eating and drinking and driving through the empty streets after curfew. Again, creating a document, you take my photo. I am so endeared to people who make me real this way.

The editors at my magazine, deciding who will take an interview. *Give it to Sam, that way we are sure to get* _____ *to do the photos.* I blush. Sure they are wrong. I have become so used to being desexualized in Vietnam, made pleasantly innocuous.

But some men have strange taste. We go on a long motorbike trip. It is maybe the most beautiful place I have been. So green. The greenest place I have ever been. My color. We follow a small clear river up a mountain, higher and deeper, until we are alone. You have somewhere to show me. A waterfall. The light twinkling.

LXXI

You have a toddler now. You treat me to bún chả, and after chè, a couples spot overrun with young lovers. My Vietnamese is so poor you laugh at me, my accent thick and you are forced to translate for me when I order. I am trying to impress you though, show you I too have things to say.

We see American films at the cinema. One night you bring your mother and brother — your mother disapproving of my bleached blonde hair, and we all sit in one long row. We hold hands.

This is not a fuck. But, this is a sweet memory. And, if we *are* only looking at photographs, this is one I like. Does it cheapen some of these to share them? I'm sure I don't really care.

LXXII

In this one I manage to retain a little dignity. Which. Considering the way I have hounded you, A., for affection and apology. Is welcome. It is welcome to feel dignified.

You are a musician and I interview you for a magazine in your home. Your presence.

One filmmaker I interview badgers me throughout the course of our conversation for my nationality, my phone number. *I just can't believe it, I've never been attracted to an American before,* etc. But otherwise, as mentioned, Vietnam has muted my sexuality and it is quite fine. I am smitten with you though as soon as you open the door. I regret intensely that I am not considered beautiful here so that I cannot have you.

Your home is a grand ecosystem off a small lake and I find it attractive that you are not like most expats hiding away in Tây Hồ. It is windows and dining tables and plants. Your son's science project. Record players and guitars. My photographer is late and so I wait to start the interview and it is just you and me. While we are still alone together you show me the library which is adjoined to the bedroom and, Jesus, the books. So many I have never seen or heard of. You are working on a project of translation. I flirt with you despite myself. When my photographer arrives I make a joke at your expense and you look at me and smile, as if you are pleasantly surprised I have any wit at all.

Weeks later I am drinking wine with a female colleague looking over the West Lake.

I am just remembering now what it felt like to have money. The self-respect granted with the ability to afford a drink or meal with a colleague. I have forgotten what it feels like to have that level of humanity. Such a small sliver of the world considered human by my own terrible logic.

A., your wife's New Year's party repulses me because it is fully people who take this for granted. It is people who are so comfortable they don't even know what to do with their privilege. Playing house in their little boxes the way they have seen it played. But, returning to this other love.

You are sitting at a table with your back to me and I catch your eye on your way out. You don't want to be a bother. You liked the article. I say, sit. Join. You are maybe a little tipsy already. You turn to my friend and tell her, *Sam is wonderful she is a wonderful listener.* My friend smiles knowingly at me. A few minutes later excusing herself, texting me, *good luck.* I am tongue-tied, trying not to bungle something so serendipitous. You begin talking about your life. Your work. We have another glass of wine, we are both drinking red. It is not common to drink wine like this in Hanoi and there is an added luxury to the evening. I am in denim. How casual a night like this seems to me I pretend. I listen.

At the end of the evening we close down the bar. It is long past curfew and the streets are empty. You offer to give me a ride. I leave my Honda Wave locked in the parking lot and climb on the back of your seat, maybe first with my hands gripping behind me, but then as we make our way around the lake, the only bike on the road, my arms move around your chest.

The advantages I am afforded here. Prancing about after curfew. They are easier to see abroad than they are at home. The history of my body pushed on the history of this nation. The knowledge marring the otherwise beautiful memory of the empty roads along the lake.

When we arrive at my alley I kiss you. I am too drunk so it is a kiss that conveys the strength of my desire in a way I was careful to conceal throughout the conversation. And this will be the dynamic of our relationship going forward. My desire for you will be boundless and I will be a curiosity to you. You will enjoy me. But, I will *want* you.

I think often of another colleague during this time. She was in her late forties, a New Yorker. *I heard you're friends with _____?* Yes I say, he's great. *Do you think he'd be interested? I think he's*, what is the word, something along the lines of *foxy* or *fine*, one that conveys explicit sexual interest. I have been dating you for several months at this point and I raise my eyebrows. I don't know, I say. I'll ask.

I am obsessed with how terrifyingly difficult it will be to find love when I am older. If I've missed my chance. You two had compatible ages. Where you were in your forties, I believe, and I was twenty-four. I'll ask, I tell her. I see myself in her want for you and I would hate to let her down.

I come over to your place in the evenings after my classes sometimes. You cook for me. Rice and egg, pour me a beer. We sit together and listen to music, or you play guitar as I write sitting in the opposite chair. You once spy over my shoulder to see what

I am working on. *I don't know if you are incubating or if you just need a push.* I am very attracted to patronizing men.

I meet your son and he is a delight. We spend time together. One night we eat dessert and I introduce you both to *Star Wars*. Your son between us on the bed, you reach out over the frame to touch my shoulder, and I hold your hand. And I can think of very few memories I have that are happier or more at peace than this.

I always want to fuck you though. I wonder still if you were attracted to me, or if whatever fleeting interest was also based on some desire for, I don't know. I am gaining weight, too many nights out keeping up with male colleagues. I want you all the time and you barely touch me at all. Once during pillow talk you make a small joke about your ex-wife and her hyper-sexuality. I know she is a dancer. I know she is very beautiful. I know you have had many lovers who are more beautiful than me. But what could I have done differently other than want you a little less?

Another list? Why not. Drinking rượu and being approved of by your friend who owns the bar, runs the city. His girlfriend praising my dress which I have designed myself with the help of a seamstress. You settling me backstage at your concert — and you come sit with me after you are done when you could be with anyone else. Spending nights with your band eating phở at 2am. The New York Times reporter at the small little venue. The books. You would give me so many books, ones impossible to find anywhere else.

It ends because I love you and you do not love me. Sitting on the floor in your apartment one night I look up at you. Maybe I should move to Istanbul?

I don't know why this is what I say. I have been doing more

work at the magazine, I have just signed another contract at my school, I am happy and content in my life. I want you to say you love me and this is the only way I know how to ask. I cannot tell you that I love you first, I cannot frighten you away like that, I cannot risk the pain. So instead I say, I think maybe I should move to Istanbul.

You look at me, and it is wrenching, you give it very little thought.

Yes, that might be good for you.

And so reader, off to Istanbul I go.

The last time I see you you are on your bicycle on Đội Cấn.

Now here, your story. The one you would write if you were the writer you wish you were. I will not do it any kind of justice here I'm sorry. Maybe I should try somewhere else or maybe it is not mine to share. I'm sure it is wrong. I am sure I do not even remember it correctly.

There is a storm in Hanoi. A typhoon. A flood. And if you have not lived in Hanoi you do not understand the weather. The rain at a horizontal driving your motorbike through streets where the dirty water comes above your handlebars some places. Praying your engine doesn't sputter out. The cold, and the hot. You are with your wife and your son is very young. Perhaps a toddler. You are overrun, afraid for your lives, forced to leave your home. You get a room in a hotel but you must still travel to find it. You wade through the flooded streets with your son on your shoulders and your wife by your side. Taking care. But when you arrive at the hotel your wife makes a call. You hear the love in her voice and know she is having an affair. And she leaves you I believe, leaves you and your son in the hotel during the storm to make sure her lover is safe.

Remembering this, whether it is accurate or not, I am. Envy. That the man she loved was worth doing this for. I am. Aghast at my own envy. Thinking of the pain, of your wife's pain A., alone with your son, just so I could have you. And still. My first feeling is one of deep guttural loathsome envy. Were I so precious to be worth it.

II

A.

Sitting with your wife and son while you cook dinner. You slit open your finger and it starts to bleed. Ah! Your wife, texting, maybe her boyfriend — how do I even begin to express my rage at her hypocrisies, my rage at your cowardice in the face of her hypocrisies, like you *want* to be controlled by her, like you *want* to hurt me just so she will never have to see herself for who she actually is, like you *want* to enable her desire for only a certain type of elite in your orbit — never looks up. Your wife never once looks at you.

You're fine just hold it above your head. At most irked by your suffering.

From the kitchen, *I think it might be deep.*

She does not look at you. *You're fine.* And you are in pain.

And I, between you two aghast, sickened by the dynamic at play.

She does not look at you once while I want to kiss the finger dry.

This is who you want so much more than me. It is not a question. This is who you want. You have told me again and again this woman is who you want. And even if you had not told me, I have seen it on your face that this is who you want. I see it in the way you speak of her with reverence. *You know nothing about my marriage.* The way you watch her when she is in the room. You watch her the way I watch you.

This woman is better than me. The world has rewarded this woman for her inherent worth with money, family, love — her every whim and pleasure. This woman right here is deserving. Despite the fact that she is selfish and sour to her core? Despite the fact that she uses you to accommodate her desires? A., do you like being used?

Perhaps she is rewarded not despite, but because of her hypocrisies. Perhaps you like that she prioritizes her own self-preservation because if you keep her company it also preserves you. Perhaps you so convincingly dress in socialist rhetoric to disguise your instincts for middle-class luxuries, the righteous young lawyers of Paris. It must make it so easy to look at yourselves in the mirror in your costumes.

But, no, she is rewarded because you just love her more.

A small orgasm here. Behind my desk a young woman gripping her own firm breasts and as soon as I start to cum a deep voice that begs me to lie on the cold floor.

He will never touch you again.

LXI

On the train in the observation car you let me eat your chocolate covered peanuts. You tell me there is real food too. I laugh. A silver fox and in the train's bathroom you take off my blouse to bite my nipples and I am embarrassed I am so dirty. To get away I pretend to fall asleep next to the woman I have given the window-seat to. You look at me, tuck a Heineken into my bag, and walk away. A note. One more for the road.

II

You do an Elvis Presley impression and point to me in my pony-tail with the red ribbon. You always point to me. I'm your girl and everyone knows it. Even when the boys draw my breasts on the board in chalk, label them, and tell the class they are the only reason you like me. I know it isn't true. You write me notes and I call you sometimes at night and when your brother answers we tease you together.

Sixth grade I sit with my friend on her sofa. And we're going to get married, and I think we'll have a farm — maybe two boys and two girls. My friend's mother overhears us. My friend's father is a writer. He reads a short story of mine and laughs. He praises my singing or my performance in a school play every time he sees me. Congratulating me too after. How many of my friend's parents raised me, fed me, one mother packing her daughter an entire second meal every day because I was always trading for extra food, growing too fast for one regular hot school lunch to sate me.

I wonder to myself how my friend's father loves his wife who is not beautiful, and old besides. I do not know anything about

women or why they could be worth loving without being pretty
and young and obliging.

My mother once. There are good times. I see how hard she was
trying. When I am maybe twelve she drives me to Spokane to
see my favorite musical. It will not be the only time she will do
this for me when I am consumed with a piece of theater. Once
we go all the way to Oregon to see a production of *King Lear*,
which I will do anything I can not to miss a production of to this
day. She will fall asleep in the second act and her contact lens
will be lost and her phone will go off during Gloucester's silence
under the tree and I will be embarrassed to be seen with her.
That poor woman.

In Spokane there is a couple who sit in front of us. I still
remember what they looked like. Both brunettes around the
same size. The woman with a chin length bob. A bit of a nose.
The man with glasses and a beard. She is poised. He is giddy —
whispering song lyrics in her ear so close the small hairs on her
cheeks and the back of her neck seem raised. She smiles at him
and the look they exchange is more graphic than any kiss. They
hold hands. He tightens his grip on her and pulls her fingers to
his lips.

My mother is, I can see it now, absolute thirst. She turns to me
and whispers. *He loves her so much.* — *He loves her so much, it
doesn't make sense. She's not even very pretty.* Maybe she is
asking me to explain the phenomenon to her. I look and I agree
with her. The woman isn't very pretty. But still, it is there.
Glaring evidence. This man is, almost indecently, in love with
this woman — despite the fact that she is not very beautiful.

I cannot see my friend's mother for her big smile and gregarious
wit and grounded joy and deep warmth and immeasurable
courage and competence. Not her generosity, even to me.

I can only see that she is gray and a little fat.

When my friend's mother hears my plans for the future she looks over and says, *you know Sam, you can do anything you want to do.*

And this has not occurred to me before. What does she mean by anything? And I revisit it often. And at the risk of sounding melodramatic or making this seem a device — it is not, it is the truest memory I have — this woman, here, makes possible for me a life. Any life.

LXXIII

You are an architect living with your parents. You are soft spoken. We kiss once on top of Galata tower. We eat breakfast and hold hands. We go to plays. I told you I will never miss a *King Lear* if I can help it. No matter how poor the quality of the production. And this one, the quality is very poor. It is joyful to watch though knowing most of the lines seeing it performed in Turkish. *Piç*, pronounced like peach. *Piç, piç, piç... piç*. As if Edmund is speaking directly to me.

V

You would hold me. Well above six foot. And big. We had
health class together and I was the new girl and we would talk
about books. I loved Plath and you Stephen King.

When I would sneak out of my house to just sit behind a dump-
ster we would plan ahead. You would come to comfort me. Just
hold me. I do not even think I was crying. Could cry. Then. I
just wanted to be held. In my neighborhood? In the dark?

You write an erotic story about me. I want to say the first time I
see myself in writing through someone else's eyes. But no. It has
happened already before. What to do with the, revulsion.
Simultaneous ego boosting flattery and disgust at the way I
behave inside of the narrative. Not my true behavior but the
behavior you desire from me. Pink lingerie. A blow job. Already
scripted and uninteresting. Don't worry I play the part good I
play the part again and again and again and again. Ad nauseam.

There is a photo of us in an ice-cream shop, drenched from
walking in the rain for hours. You envelop me completely so all

you can see is the back of my hair, my dripping black hoodie.
My eyes are closed.

The desire for containment or closeness. Is it a desire for seclusion? For safety? Or is the desire for entrapment.

I watch videos of women duct-taped from head to foot. Crying.
Screaming. But. Contained.

XXIX

Here A. This is the first one I write for you. I write it to show you, to ask you to be careful with me. Perhaps it was unfair.

I do not know it is a date. Later you tell me about female students who are your friends, like sisters or daughters. I wonder why I could not have been one of them. I even ask you this, years later, the last time you consent to conversation. Why was that not me?

This first time I meet you off-campus to talk about writing, maybe the first time I've gone to center city alone — sweating newness and womanhood. Maybe my third or fourth sit-down dinner that isn't Olive Garden. You buy me pasta and have a glass of wine at noon, which I have never seen anyone do and I am thrilled. Too nervous to eat I take the full portion home in a little box. I remember almost nothing of the conversation but I remember the panels of light. I remember thinking I was doing so well, how smart you must find me. Eighteen in my first semester and you say my papers are already graduate level. *What a progressive mind.*

Even this first time I believe you mention your father, then your book, then your girlfriend who is living somewhere else. Maybe California which makes me think she must be tall and busty and blonde. You are the same age as my father but so different. So alive. You were charismatic and charming in the classroom but now to have this all to myself? It is unbearable. That you should find me clever and grown-up enough to spend this hour with.

You take the train back to campus with me and we sit side by side. At first I am focused on trying not to allow my body to touch your body in any way. An inch between us. So as not to offend. But then I am focused on trying to find something to say. You have stopped talking.

I am wearing a mini-skirt. I feel a mass on my knee. It is you. It is your hand. Not just my knee, my thigh. The inside of my thigh.

I want to die. It is not exaggeration. Nausea and fear that over-whelms me, heightened due to my youth, as strong as I have ever felt it. Writing this now I feel it. Panic. The desire to vomit up not just the content of one's stomach but one's very ability to perceive, to exorcise one's very life force. I do nothing. I am frozen. You leave the hand there, I cannot remember how long. I am captive. The pasta sitting on my lap covering my crotch. I am grateful for the protection.

Arriving on campus you ask if I would like to go back to your office. I would not. I would like to go to my 7-11 and buy candy bars and do my homework with the television on loud. I would like to shower. I would like to be far away from both our bodies, existing only in a cerebral dimension.

But, I do not say no. It is such a generous invitation after all. I switch. Here I question myself. You do not coerce me. You have suggested to me how things will proceed, and I am not as ignorant or stupid as all that. I must know what will happen. And I change my mind. We go back to your office.

In the elevator we stand behind another of my English professors, a gentle older man. He smiles at me and watches as I get off with you. I tell myself he cannot know, but the memory haunts me for the next four years as I take several more classes with him. I wonder if he guesses our secret.

In the office you leave the door cracked open for appearances. I feel sickly envious at the academic squalor. I sit across from you and every time I sit across from someone in this way I have this memory. Visceral. In therapists' offices and at job interviews and when I meet with my thesis advisors. So that I blush sometimes. So that I cannot open my mouth or else it will be taken wrong. So I grow irrationally angry. When I meet with my own students, it is always in public, always with a table between us so that they are protected.

We sit like this, student and teacher, and you touch my knees again. You pull out a flask. *Would you like a drink?* I shake my head. No. I don't want to get in trouble. I say this. You say, *I thought you liked to drink.* I do, I say, I am a very good drinker. I say this. You say no one will know. I cannot remember if I have a drink, but I know you do. You smell like it. This memory is whiskey and old books and spring air from the open window so if someone were tall enough they could see in.

You pull me onto your lap. Pull. I remember sitting on your lap but I do not remember how I got there. In memory I seem so small but I do not know what I felt at the time. Maybe bloated and red and oversized as I often feel. Maybe afraid of you seeing me close up. Maybe just sick. When I see this image I see someone younger than their age. How odd and wrong it seems in memory and how commonplace it might have been — my naked legs resting on one of your thighs. I remember this now still, the door open, or did you close it? Eighteen when we met but now nineteen. So an adult.

Reading this I am afraid of you laughing. Nineteen and thirty-eight (I believe). Not so bad at all. Not the biggest age gap in my life. Not the most egregious imbalance of power. And I such a robust nineteen and experienced and convinced of my adult-hood. Then why? Reading do you think me a snowflake, that this should haunt me, terrify me, become a concrete part of my identity. That of ingenue. That of temptress. When I was looking for someone to see me. How much harder it has made it to believe myself human.

I remember now you are not even my teacher. It is Spring semester and I took your class in the fall. Why did you email me? Why did I respond? Yahoo will not let me access my account, and I try. Two days of calling and emailing. All dust then. So even more reason for you, reader, to see this as a love affair. Nothing more than two consenting adults. Laugh me off this page for suggesting anything different.

When I go home, I cry. I tell my roommate who tells me sternly to not be that girl. I tell the boy I am sleeping with who tells me to ignore you — but he leaves me soon after and I forget to take his advice. I tell my ex-boyfriend from high-school. He laughs. I showed him the poem you gave me in class however many months before, the Carver in which Bukowski drinks and fucks his student and does not rhyme and is not romantic. He says he knew then.

Then, why didn't I.

The next time we meet I do not know but I imagine it will be sex. I am not as young as all that. You are not the first older man who has sat me on their lap. So why then am I nervous? Why then am I not certain? What am I holding out for. Do you see how unreliable I am as narrator?

I spend my student loan money on lingerie. A seventy dollar padded bra I still have today, a decade old but mostly unused. Stockings. You tell me you liked watching me uncross my legs in miniskirts and stockings in class. I am startled to learn I was being watched.

But see, I must have known how this night would be.

Still, I remember, and I do not think I was certain.

You take it for granted that I know how to eat out. You buy a bottle of wine for the table on a little patio near the train station. I mimic how you hold the glass, I do not know if I had held one before. You live in the suburbs and I am conscious on the train that when I arrive I will be trapped if we stay out too late. I order a salad but I cannot eat it. I've taken laxatives all week so you will think I am beautiful. So I will fit into my new denim skirt which I have bought, will buy, to impress you. Do I wear it for this meeting or later? Too thin but still we struggle to get it off me. A single lettuce leaf would disrupt my empty system which I have made sterile for you. I drink. You talk.

Partway through the night, I do not know when — I remember now how readily you would touch me, on my bare shoulders, my hands, gestures of affection I had not been shown with this level of authority — you tell me, you say it gently asking for my permission without explicitly asking, that you have booked a room at a bed and breakfast nearby.

I am nervous to be naked in front of you, that you will be disappointed. As we have seen I am used to fucking but I have just started dating senior undergraduates who want to go slow, who want to look at me rather than push me onto their cock in an

empty parking lot. So I am prepared, but I am terrified as you
undress me, cursing as you do — angrily but with what I recognize is pleasure at what you are seeing, which is my essence, my
shell, my secret. I lie down on the bed.

I don't know what else to do. Unmarked and small, I am scandalized by the memory of this and cannot fathom how you could
bear to touch it. How did it not burn to the touch. How are you
not scarred from the scalding heat of its youth.

And then you undress yourself.

I have never seen a man as old as you without clothes on, and
your body disgusts me. I am sorry even now to offend, but it
does. You have more weight to you than I knew and it is all
around the middle and arms. Your cock is still flaccid. It is
summer and you have been sweating all night, your body slick
with it. The lights are on and you are red and hairy and covered
in moles. You are big and old and I am already naked on the bed
and have already consented to this but feel abject horror at the
thought of you near me, inside of me.

I think you kiss me.

You try to eat me, but I am scandalized at the thought. That you
should see even more of me. That you might feel revulsion at
the taste of me, the same revulsion that I feel at the sight of you.
I do not remember all the steps. I remember you on top of me in
missionary, crushing me, not the adept lover I'd been anticipating but clumsier than a teen. I am dry and you offer lube. I
interpret it as insult. I am cold but after you are done and in the
bathroom I have to wipe your sweat off of my body. You do not
last long but it is ages as I try to find the room to breathe from
under you. Thinking of you in my belly.

Afterwards though, you hold me gratefully and I feel wanted

and endeared to you again, shocked that you would choose me. We go out for more wine. I feel beautiful when I am drunk and feeling beautiful improves my mood. There is a wedding at the hotel that weekend. The weather is perfect and the moon is full and there is a decorated patio made up for the happy couple. Empty though. The party moved elsewhere, but still music is playing.

You dance with me. And despite all this I still find that moment beautifully romantic, like a movie. A perfect story. We sway and I fit against you. I feel so lucky.

We go back to the room.

My mother once told me a story about her honeymoon. She was sixteen and my father eighteen. A gorgeous young couple. They went to a ski-lodge to celebrate after the ceremony which was attended by nearly the entire high school, so crowded that they ran out of food within an hour. I do not know what compelled my mother to tell me this, we are not close, but she was not happy on the honeymoon. She woke up in the middle of the night and missed her family, her home. She was still a child sleeping in a bed with a man, even one she had chosen, even one almost as young as she — and she said, maybe not in these exact words, that she was very afraid.

I was present on that honeymoon, still invisible, inside the womb. Genderless and warm. Perhaps I inherited that sadness though. That displacement. That too early adulthood. Sometimes I ache with homesickness despite the fact I very rarely have had a home.

I think of that first night sleeping with you. Sick with longing for something and not knowing what it was, facing away from you, moving my ass further from the powdery fragile skin of your cock and balls but my head closer to your arm and heart.

This inheritance of women.

I google you out of habit. Obsessively. Monthly. Weekly. Some weeks daily. Some days, hourly. Like with you A. You two draw me into compulsions.

I approach men reading in coffee shops around the world who have nothing more than your posture, just to check the expression of their faces when they see me, not completely sure I would be able to recognize you after all this time.

And you have changed. I find a picture from your wedding. You are trimmer. You smile broadly. You are in a pink tie on a beach. A beach wedding. You. That you are such a stranger to me after all.

From this night we begin an affair that lasts through the summer, though it felt so much longer. At least once a week you get a hotel room. Sometimes we go to the ballet first. Sometimes we eat. Always we drink. Two or three bottles of wine. I do not know if they were good. I cut my hair short to feel more womanly. I ride you often as you like to watch. I wear the bracelet everyday which you bought me in Europe where you were on holiday with your girlfriend.

I do not know if you tell me you have broken up with her or if I invent this narrative, but I remember the night you turn to me and ask, ... *have you been the other woman before? You seem so experienced.* Almost like a joke. I have not. I do not even know that is what I am doing then. As you see reader I will be again though. A masochistic and unethical habit I just cannot shake, to be nothing more than that bit on the side.

But, if I was lying to myself, I believe you must have helped. I remember the first night I was allowed to visit you in your apartment. Maybe a month in. Full of old bric a brac from the seventies and literary journals and both dingier and more adult than I'd imagined. That night was the best night. A good night. That night we ate frozen ravioli and I licked the plate clean and we argued about a single Ralph Ellison sentence smoking on your porch and I told you I loved you and I think, I am not sure, that you said you loved me back. That night I came out of your bathroom holding a Clinique night cream. Whose is this? *My mother visited*, you said. Maybe that was true. But, maybe the lie was not all my fault. Maybe all I did was consent to the narrative you'd created, not invent it entirely. I did not think it was a face cream for a woman your mother's age.

Washing. This too. I think this is the night you tell me about your OCD. Is it the night or is it when we are in the car the next day? You are tapping at, if I remember, a Wookiee hanging from the mirror. You lament Catholicism. Before you eat chocolate chip pancakes for breakfast. I am always amazed at how frequently you are able to eat. We sit in the car in the parking lot of a baseball field afterwards. This memory so vivid. The car is hot and I am disheveled. I cannot remember if you told me before or is it here about your mother, the divorce and near suicide. I believe this is the first time you tell me fully about mental illness and isolation. So that years of your life are gone and now I think how strange that we would have so many of the same symptoms, and that I would too be here in my life. And why is that connection there? And why does it take my breath away to think of it?

Again, the girlfriend returns to the story, as a caregiver. But you imply somewhere else, I am sure, that now she is gone. Then, in the same breath. *She can never find out.*

You are yet to go on your book tour. I remind myself of this constantly and when I take three steps back I see quite clearly. I was a just dessert after the meal of publishing. I was a reward, a treat after so many difficult years of asceticism and pain. I was never a person to you.

You write a poem about me when we are first seeing each other. You write two poems about me that I am aware of, each startlingly off the mark in their own unique ways. In the first one you call me Samantha, as though you only know my name through MLA format or a class roster and not, as is the truth, through acquaintance. In the poem you say I have always lived in a city, which having shared with you the fact that I spent my childhood in Idaho, is remarkably forgetful. I believe you cite my eyes as the incorrect color. In the second poem you compare me to food at a small American buffet. You cite my curves, of which I have almost none. I revive you by calling you a genius, which I may very well have done in those days. You undress me, publicly.

The amount to which you romanticized me then. I wonder were I to see you again how disappointed you would be, if I would have to see the pity in your eyes as you must have seen it in mine that first night. I have considered this when I have considered visiting you in your office, forcing you to engage with me. This is the consideration that always stops me. Certainly I am less beautiful now and I cannot bear for you to see it. This, and the fear of seeing through the crack in your door a teenager on your lap.

Still. It is only a summer. Retrospectively such a small time and such a small love affair. My obsession even still shows how capable I am of the pathological — the pathetic. I move to Japan in August. Not even a full summer.

Towards the end things begin to deteriorate. We spend two hours in the afternoon at a dingy brown motel on the side of a highway. I am very afraid of you this day. I think because we do not drink. I dance around your grabbing hands while singing show tunes. I do not know why this is what I do. I never say no to you. I have only very recently learned, and not very well, that no is something I am allowed to say. This afternoon makes you very angry, but you do not treat me poorly. Perhaps you are angry because this is the afternoon you realize you are sleeping with someone still very young.

This is the last hotel for a while, but you sleep over at my apartment the day before we take a trip to NYC where I am getting my visa for Tokyo. I am alone as all my other roommates are spending the summer with their families. Perhaps because I am excited, or more confident in my own space, I drink with abandon. We do not both fit on the bed, so straddling me on the floor you ask me to touch myself. I do not believe I have ever done this for someone before. I do not touch myself when I am alone yet and feel nothing but shame while you watch from above, stroking. Around now is when something breaks in me. Do I cry first, or vomit.

This is the first time in years I remember I was raped. We have seen scenes like this later in my life, but here for you reader, the first time.

I had to go back. Help me. I don't want to go back. This has been so tightly held as a secret to me. I tell you now though, half naked and shaking and covered in regurgitated red wine. I howl. It is animal. I revile the memory, of how many lovers and strangers have been forced to sedate me in this state. I recoil from myself. But, as I said, this is the first time. This is when I break open.

Do I curse you, or thank you? How much longer might it have stayed dormant in me. What if I had managed to never let it out at all? Kid stuff. I think you might say this to me when I tell you I am heartbroken over my ex. Why then do you take this seriously? Why do you stay the night and do you feel anything besides trapped? Are you starting to see me? These indignities that gave me the lived experience to feel confident in your grace? Do you see my pain as kid stuff? I cannot. I cannot comprehend the logic. I try and try and, you, I cannot comprehend.

I sleep through the scheduled first train to the city. I wake late and see you on my roommate's old bed on the other side of the room. I have vomit on my face and hair but I believe you have taken off some of the dirty clothes. Maybe that was not you. Maybe that was someone else in some other time on a similar morning. Yes, dear reader. There were many of them.

We do not talk about it. You are angry though. I wear a mini-skirt. I wear a blouse with cherry blossoms on it as the visa office is going to take my picture. I pack my bag with disposable cameras and Murakami books and a sweater. You take a photo of me at 30 Rock in front of the statue of Atlas. Posing. I take a photo of you in front of a cathedral, but I do not know in which book I hide it. It was the only one of you I had.

At the station you buy us both tickets and this is the most money I have ever seen someone spend on me like this. One hundred dollars or so. The memory of you signing your name when you pay for them is perhaps the strongest in this whole tale, whatever that says about me. You tell me I hold up with the New York women but do not say that I am pretty.

On the train we are our best. We are both reading and you put your arm around me. I love trains and we talk softly about the landscape, about New York. It is one of the few memories I have of us in public. Acting a couple.

I have not been to NYC since fifteen when a friend and I stole her father's credit card to drink green apple Zima's and cavort in orange mini dresses. The night ending in us being mistaken by two older Australians for something that can be bought. Smoking outside of the hotel and one man catches onto our ages sooner than the other, pulling his companion away. So, I am pleased to feel so, rich, with you. It is not until the end of the day of hot dogs and sight-seeing that you mention the previous night. *Do you remember?* You ask me. *Do you remember what you said?*

We are at the train station. We are standing at a staircase. There is a large clock. I remember these things clearly, but I do not remember what I say.

We take the train home and I believe I spend the night alone in the empty apartment trying to clean red wine out of the carpet and watching Star Trek Voyager to keep away thought. I believe I watch television every hour I am alone for the next two years, to keep from saying out loud, sober, I was raped.

Why did you not hold me if you loved me. Why did you tell me to get help, but then leave. Why do I mention this night at all, or attach you to this other narrative, only because you were present? Am I saying you are complicit in the same system as a rapist? Who at least proposed after the indignity. Whose name I can sometimes tolerate, when I cannot bear the taste of yours? That you were both inadvertently or actively agents of torture, I cannot decide.

In which of these essays am I making myself a victim? Reader, where in this book do I take away my own agency?

I have read this one many times to myself looking for the where, the when, the moment things could have gone differently. Searching for what I ought to answer for so I am not casting blame where it does not belong.

Reader, what am I?

The night before I leave for Japan you pick me up from my parents' place. My parents, my father who is one year younger than you, sit inside while you pick me up. I have a silk slip on under my clothes and we pull into a hotel in town. I think we hold each other more than we have sex. I think this night I believe you will miss me.

You tell me about your high-school sweetheart who sent you a bit of her pubic hair in an envelope. I laugh at you. You might cry. You try to explain to me, this is important. *Don't you know love like this is once in a lifetime?* Once. And I do not believe you. It haunts me. A., until you I doubted I could feel this way, certain I would never again love like this. Incapable. The you of the two of you sliding back and forth, forward and back so slippery I am left unsettled and lost. That I could fall again and again for more of the same.

Our two bodies in the bed. The window. The small-town noises outside. Returning home and finishing packing my bags, opening my passport, and looking at the surly photo on the visa. Wondering if I would see you again but never once thinking I would be here, now.

Then, reader, is this a love story? If not reader. What story is this.

XXX

Just a few days after the hotel, across the world, you are the next person I fuck. You have his same name spelled just with one extra letter and no professor preceding it. Still it feels the same on my tongue and that sameness feels good. It staunches the missing. You are in your mid-twenties and so calm and distinctive from the mass of twittering boys and girls in the hotel lobby where we meet. The first time we have sex you say, *there is so much more that we get to do. We have so much more time.*

I become too attached. Just one week. Two. Already I am obsessed with you. I write you poems and club more than you like and ask you to join and I am frantic with the city. I am. Up. I am. Delighted. I cannot sleep or I will not be able to see enough, desperate to distract myself. Meanwhile you have been preparing for years and you consume slowly and with consciousness. Your careful Japanese. Translations on your nightstand. You do not want to go to Harajuku with me again. You just need a night to focus on your kanji and there isn't enough time for sex too. *Why can't we try the jazz cafe around the corner instead of going all the way to Shibuya?* Fronting me money for karaoke none of my funds have been deposited. Photos of us smoking together. The same cool posture, the same expression.

I listen to a podcast now where a woman hits her rock bottom sitting outside of a man's door, a kitchen knife to her wrist, cutting every time he refuses to say he loves her. She tells us listeners, *if you do the work there is a way to retain your dignity. I do not know what you do with the pain,* she tells us, *but there is a way to retain some version of yourself you can bear to look at.*

I pound on your door, Please, please, please. Calling your name. That same name still, hot and rough from my throat. We know who I wanted. A female friend collecting me while I sob. Taking me to my room. She tells me, *you're acting a little crazy.*

My second day in Tokyo I convince several people that since Mt Fuji is closing for the season this is our opportunity to climb. I do not even have a winter coat. I have filled my suitcase with boxes of tampons, silk dresses, my favorite black / blue hair dye. We take a bus the next morning and I am woefully unprepared in leopard print ballet flats. My first bowl of udon soup in a cafeteria at the base of the mountain. Making friends with a pair of girls from Hong Kong on the bus. I am so chatty. I am so eager. Halfway up the mountain we are too cold and lost besides. We did not bring our own lights. It is a deep desolate dark and I have never exercised a day in my life and many of us are so cold we are blue. Two of our companions go on ahead but you stay to make sure the rest of us are safe. Sitting with the security near their small space heater until the sun has risen and we can find our way back down.

The look in your eyes that night, one of resigned disappointment.

That care should be sacrifice. I'm not sure.

For you too A. Are they synonymous? Should they be?

XXXIII

Before you fuck her you fuck me. At a party in a penthouse a group has rented on the top floor of a hotel. Floor to ceiling windows so you can see all of Tokyo spreading around you and away and it is impossible to feel less significant than you do confronted with this view. I'm smoking chocolate cigarettes with a group of men but follow you into a bathroom. I've heard the joke before, you have an aquatic dick. Is the shower running or is the bath half filled up? I'm still smoking. Not even completely undressed. Riding you. Your thick amiable face and shoulders beneath me. Your hands moving my hips.

And I can hear _____ at the door. *Please. Please don't.* And I like it. The sudden reversal.

Coming out my clothes wet and everyone has heard. One of my friends pulling me close, *how was it honey?* And an earthquake. Stirring the party for a moment. Glasses tipping a porno falling off of a table the city continuing to sprawl beneath us.

After the Big One many of you trickle back to Philadelphia, all with the tell-tale signs of trauma. It is too much to be on the train. Sudden noises. You describe the rolling of the asphalt. The relentlessness of the wait.

Back. A few days later. You buy me a pizza. It is sex.

Sometimes I walk past your room and can hear the two of you together. I imagine you touching her body. The way she prefers your touch to mine.

You later will publish a small poetry chapbook about your time in Tokyo. I'm sure I have no interest in it.

XXXI

I suppose you must have fucked me from behind? I know I
fucked you, oh a few times. Also in Nikko so the German
staying with us could not get into the room. You are blonde,
arrogant, and unkind.

You are the one who tells me they're fucking each other. In such
detail. *They both have told each other they didn't much care for
your (my) body.* On a train. In front of the only friend I have not
fucked, who does not know I am such a slut. And she looks at
me and asks, *all of them?*

Five years later in Seoul the first thing you will say to me is,
*some men might like the weight, you gained so much, especially
in your ass.* Makgeolli, soju, a two piece punk band that give me
a T-Shirt. You pawn me off on a friend who eats me and fingers
me but who I will not let fuck me because I know he is engaged.

In the morning I take a cab to the airport and sleep alone in
Kunming.

XXXV

I come to in a McDonalds making out with a man who has
followed me home from a club. It is maybe somewhere between
2am and 5am, neon signs the only light. The streets empty. The
second floor of the restaurant is full of sleepers. When I snap
into myself I look at the man who I have just been kissing and
am afraid. I tell him to leave me alone. I run out the McDonalds
and down the streets towards my apartment and he starts to
chase me. I run faster fumbling for my phone. You pick up and
you meet me outside our building. Pull me inside. Confront the
man. Tell him to leave.

I do not know how to explain this scene. Who the man was or
what his intentions were in following me. I was slipping in and
out of myself so much those days, sober too, not just in the night.
One day holding a red balloon I found on the road and placing
it in my left arm like it is my baby and wandering down the
streets of Tokyo. Showing it the sights. And sometimes it was a
fun game for people with me. Like it was an affect. Like I was
putting on a show.

But this night is not a fun game but a frightening one and you let me stay in your room. You say I know it is scary and you tell me it will be okay. You let me curl in a ball on your floor until it is morning and then we go to class. We have sex, I am almost sure another day. I am quite sure you are always very kind to me.

XI

The first exchange we have that is just the two of us you ask me if I know what the words mean in my lines. The specific line said to the group of boys — what do you think this is, some kind of gang bang? You ask. *Do you even know what a gang bang is?*

The first conversation we have that is just the two of us is about porn. You are showing me how to roll a joint in a parking lot outside of a diner talking about watching a woman get fucked by a horse. And how exciting it is. How much she wants it.

_____ is in love with you. Almost everyone is in love with you though. Wickedly smart and funny and when Green Day is looking for a bassist at a show they pick you. Always high. You would tell me you want me but I would not believe you. And _____ would be so jealous. I play with a few of the boys she wants. Not because I want them, but because I want her, and I hate that she won't want me back. I think she sees your cock first. Maybe sucks it. Reports to me. It is disappointing. Small. Which seems so rude.

And so my first time is not painful. It is not emotional. It is quite

And so my first time is not painful. It is not emotional. It is quite fine.

Well, there is the first time and then there is the first time. There are all the times where we grind in the woods between our apartments and you bend me over benches or trees and say, *would it ruin your day if I had sex with you right now?* And I say, maybe, and so we never do. But the first time is in your room and we've decided ahead. You pick me up after school, my new high school on the other side of town. We go up to your room and you bend me over a coffee table. I've never since been so wet. You pump yourself inside me, I can hardly feel it. It feels like so much less than three or four fingers which you've previously allowed me. Then you are done. Maybe not even three thrusts. The soundtrack is the White Stripes and I use Kleenex after Kleenex between my thighs trying to dry myself. Running still with more want, except you are already sated. I'm not sure we kiss or otherwise touch, before, or after.

And the first time after that is a snow day. I remember it being Valentines but maybe I am aggrandizing it. Neither of us have school and we have your place to ourselves. You pour me orange juice. I don't remember which music you choose. This time you last longer and we don't just resign ourselves to one position but instead explore many. I did not know there were so many positions. In your living room with the windows open so we can see the snow. We use the sofa. We use the floor. I am so insecure of my body. I am cold. But it is not a bad memory. I remember thinking, I like this.

Taking your cock in my mouth you tell me there is a kind of woman who when she sucks a cock looks like she really wants it, needs it, and you want me to be that type of woman when I grow up. I say, teach me how.

I wonder sometimes what it would have been like to have loved someone. But, not often. Once, maybe twice. Now. Thinking of you A. I wonder. But I do not think I could have done it that way. And you were not aggressive but instead quite allowing, eager to explore with my permission. Which I gave you very willingly. A very good first time.

We keep in touch for many years after. You regale me with tales from your life as a musician in LA. Once you visit me in Philly and I introduce you to _____ and the three of us get plastered and you drive us along the highway swerving four lanes left and right while I sit on someone's lap barely breathing. After you fuck me and scratch deep into my skin so that I scream.

XXXIV

The First Woman I Fuck

[Redacted. Mine.]

LXXIV

The Woman I Want to Marry

[Redacted. Also mine.]

A.

It is tiresome, isn't it. Madonna / Whore. Saint / Jezebel. Those women — and this woman.

And we know who they are, who this woman is.

Reader. We certainly know what I am.

A., I hate your wife and I know it makes me even more of a cliché. I promise I have tried very hard not to. She's not as smart as she thinks she is. She parrots what she has heard very well but she cannot keep up when things move outside the lines. Still, you believe her. She is sheltered and small. She is cruel and cold and feels entitled to everything.

Our first date you say she sends you off with a smile.

Good luck.

A. You are so sweet seeming. I am inclined here to use the vocabulary that I used for that first essay. I write it the same way because I meet you and you remind me of him often very early,

and even more now. You use his same lines without even knowing. You are his best qualities — the gregarious charm and wit
and humor, the understanding of pain. This book is yours. But
no, you're right, mostly it is yours, but, not *just* yours A. Not just
yours and yours (his). Nor is it belonging to all of these yours as
a frankenstein mass. Not each of you as individuals now
becoming a joint being but instead it belongs to the "you" of
how all of you really were always the same. You cannot combine
what is already a part. When you leave me you tell me the same
thing that you said, and you said, and you said even before that.

And us too. I am as shallow and stupid as your wife. As insecure. As desperate for your attention.

And one of the reasons I am writing this is to face the consequences of my actions, pretending again I am separate and
unique in order to give myself permission to tell these stories.
You are all horrid consequences. You are all pain. However,
there is no pretense at victimization in this story A. Here I
cannot pretend I am not a part of birthing the pain. Accommo-
dating its birth.

Her form. Convex and brimming.

Letting her fill and dip deeper under the weight alone in order
to keep you longer for myself.

That first night it is so encouraging that you are so trustworthy.
Mature. Eleven years with your wife who is older than you and
who you admire, you speak of her so highly and without a hint
of condescension. It is the middle of January. I have just the
week before moved back to the city from Chicago and the
weather is well below freezing, maybe below zero. The bar is
small, a speakeasy on top of an Ethiopian restaurant and while I
could not even find the entrance you are a familiar here. The
black spider hanging from the ceiling and the torn office furni-

ture. I remember watching you stand at the bar, something strangely earnest about the posture — the legs spread a little leaning forward. Not a particularly tall man but steeped in belonging and so the place lends you stature. Grace. The word for you is grace. When I find out you are a "real" writer, the blush in my cheeks of embarrassment to have been speaking so freely, so confidently.

You are not much older than me but you are so much fuller. You have a home in the city, a book, you know the bartender. I kiss you goodnight and I like the shape of your lips so much they are so sweet and so warm. Later I google your wife, preoccupied since our first conversation with how intimidatingly lovely she must be to be so adored by you. I am ashamed when I first see her to say I am relieved that I am prettier than her. Maybe it is the almost decade between us but maybe not. Maybe she is more elegant, maybe more unflinching in her beauty — but I am at least prettier. Maybe even more interesting. She is a schoolteacher with a square jaw and gray hair. And at first the fact that you love this woman makes me trust you even more.

The first time with me, you say it has been ten years and you are nervous, and I am trying to be calm. I am trying to show you sex means nothing with me. Just a fun time. I may even tell you this to try and calm your nerves, which I am worried are actually evidence of a lack of desire. The first time you see my cunt, *those lips*, as if you have forgotten there are bodies that are not shaped like hers. And we are so clumsy at first — how we ever managed.

It is required that I meet your wife early for our tryst to be allowed. "Allowed." This is not what I had anticipated. I had not anticipated so many small rules. When you tell me your wife falls in love with men and fucks men and goes on long international holidays with men and is happily shared by you, I think you will be shared easily with me too. Not so. The first requirement is that I visit your home to be appraised.

Your wife keeps us waiting. A blatant lie. I am late. Still her presence is one of control. You show me your house. Huge. Four stories and a grand piano and a yard and a kitchen which you've re-done and a parlor and an office in the attic. Your wife comes down the staircase with one hand on the bannister. She looks older than my mother and aunts — closer to their age than mine — and more regal than a duchess. She sits at a chair behind an open New Yorker at a large round table. Her book is on the table as well with the spine facing so I can see that she authored it. She may as well have worn her tiara. She may as well have cocked her plume. She may as well have spread her knives.

I feel wonderful writing this bitter lonely garbage.

The way you talk A., I still listen to your voice. A recording of one of your stories looped so much it has become its own neural path. I've never heard a more musical voice, just the tone I would love on its own, but the content too? After the first leaving when you return to me we sit at bars and you tell me about your son and I tell you about my lovers and the stories I am engaged in and the weather, your family, my family — pains all the way down. We watch the news — another Guinness, another Jameson— and the days pass like that and there is never enough time to learn everything there is to learn. Your mind works in a way I am soothed by. Your mind is like a bowl where I am allowed to be the soup — spread in all directions and you catch me at the edges and lead me back and say, *you may spill over a bit but, come, you are allowed to settle.* Look how warm we keep each other. How clear and, together, how useful. The way you talk to me is pure sustenance.

This second time — after the baby — we tell ourselves we will only touch through the mind. Before the second leaving. We tell

ourselves we can forgo the body and respect the wife, the
mother, the beloved, until we are, is it us? Is it my fault? Am I
the one overtaken? Holding you that first time after so many
months and my body did not even know it was so hungry
before it.

If I find — another of you A. Another "you" again. Another
wounded writer in the throes of an existential or mid-life crisis
— when I am the same age as you and on equal footing (if it is
not foolish to hope I will ever be on similar footing) — will I still
love you? Will I be able to bear these traits that have so
endeared me? Will I fall fast and hard and again be the fool?
How bad will it hurt? If it is worse. How will I... if it is worse the
question is how will I not.

And when I am older if I am lucky enough to be tied to this
third "you" in every way — will you find someone desperate and
younger, prettier enough than me who will suck your cock for
free? Will I beg you not to let them?

Karmic. I deserve nothing less. I hope this young person in the
future writes something horrid about me. A ballad to my
growing waistline. The pithiness of my prose. My overly large
emotions and small breasts. My poor complexion. My drinking.
My wrinkles. My moods and tantrums. Let us always tear each
other apart for the abundant resource of perfectly mediocre
perfectly almost loving "nice" men.

Yet, still I wonder. What can I do to be sure I catch your eye?

The first conversation we have all sitting at the table. The topic
is the question of consent between instructors and their of-age
students. I could not make up something so obvious if I tried.
And your wife. Unsure. Unsure where the line is, and I do not
fight her. Or, I push against her a bit and after say, I am sorry. I
say it too many times in the conversation. She is stern with me

in her low staccato voice. So different from yours A. *Stop apologizing.* The way rich women like to tell poor women fetching them goods at department stores or bars, *stop apologizing and just fix it.* My mother here again, older women at the church, older men, her friends. _____ *stop saying you're sorry,* her tears already starting again and the words tumbling forth.

Stop being sorry. Like she is my better. A queen. No, a true matron.

Your wife A.? Or your mother? Sitting at the table and she "jests" once, *is it your mother you've married after all?* As if she does not realize this may cut too close to the quick.

I should not judge. It seems plenty fine to be loved by a mother.

It is funny that I am writing this essay to you, about her. She was present as often as you were. You brought her with you every time. All the conversations about her needs and well-being and distress. When I thought your love was growing for me, I was merely something to distract you from her. How could you have pretended to love me and how could I have believed you? I knew what I was walking into and yet you were so tender. My body a dry sponge. Love in every capillary so I became a shape I did not know I had the potential to grow into.

Seeing her holding your son. You invoke this image often to me, asking me to be gentle, to have pity. *What else could I do?*

And of course, you are right and good. Of course you are.

I told you I could not meet the boy, that the loss of him and you would be too much together. You pushed. The first time rocking him in my apartment and listening to the Beatles. The low bounces I remember from my childhood of caretaking. Your son's open mouth. A., your loving laughter.

You tell me you want me in your life no matter what. Verbatim. You tell me you want me in your son's life.

But, before the boy. She prefers you to have sex with me only in the afternoons. Only months later are you transparent about this. What I thought was passion was simply her pulling my strings.

She gives you a bedtime. Ten o'clock. You tell me early how autonomous the two of you are, that you have completely different lives and love it. Still. She is very cross with you if you are out past ten, even by a few minutes.

You are not permitted to stay the night. You are not permitted to introduce me to friends until she approves. At one point she vetoes me completely. Overnight I am nothing, the first time this happens. And then she changes her mind. My life usable like that. I let her do it to me too. I could have walked away, and I do not. When I come to the house she is petulant and bratty. The first night you invite me for dinner she asks me to do the dishes while she curls herself into your arms in the backyard. I learn later she does not do housework but instead merely delegates. I should admire her craftiness but cannot find anything to warrant her grandiosity. Although she is the one who wants the child it is clear you will be the parent. You will be responsible. I cannot help but wonder what you love in her. What you love about a woman won't clean her own mess.

You ask me to have empathy for her insecurities. You, reading this book, do you not feel for her? Home alone? I told you she is the good woman so feel for her all you want. This is my limit. This is the threshold of compassion I cannot cross.

I have compressed the hour you tell me you love me, and the hour you tell me she is pregnant, into the same walk in late spring. There is a large cemetery and a dirt path whose trail suits our meandering conversations. It can't possibly be the same day though, because you are sad when you tell me you love me. It is a tragedy that you love me. They must not be the same day because you are not only sad when you tell me your wife is pregnant, you are also scared.

I know that day, or those two days as one day, that I love you furiously and that it will end badly for me. End in tears. And it does. So I am not all stupid, just mostly. Willfully naive or masochistic. Too in love with pain? If you read this you must assume that, yes. I am.

This first time you leave me your wife is very pregnant. Again reader, I know where your sympathies should fall and I do not fault you. Give your sympathies to her because I cannot.

The timeline is almost identical, her pregnancy and our relationship. I am so selfish. The timing seems so cruel to me.

Why can I not place the blame where it belongs. Why must I love you so much that I forgive you and attach to her, to myself, all the fault.

You help me move into my apartment, sweating.

Don't. Go.

Don't.

And the first time you leave, you do it so suddenly. Both times it is sudden. A shock to me. The first time is just an email. You do not leave an avenue for contact or questions. I do not know what I have done wrong. I pray it is her who has drafted the text, that it is her and not your sterile words without a breath of heat in them. Freezing. I read the words so often those months in the

fall without you that I have even the punctuation still
memorized.

Let me return to flogging your wife — it is giving me so much
power. It is filling me up with righteous vitriol to make her the
witch and you the whipped little cuck.

Standing here I see you reader have found an easy path to
concern for her. That way is poison to me. It burns me even to
look at it.

I have never been so vulnerable in bed with someone. Never in my
life. So encouraged to feel desire. And I want your cock in my
mouth the most — a sex act that can feel so vile and demeaning with
others. I trust and love you so much. I want to taste you. I want to
feel you hard and close, so intimate I cannot think of anything but
what I am doing. I do not want to slide outside my body along the
walls. I do not want to look away. I cum bending over you taking you
down my throat. I have never felt so safe with a partner. We drink
beers in the shower and I beg you to fuck me on your way to work or
on your lunch break or whenever I can have you. At first you insist
you like it gentle. You need it slow, allotting time for you to finger
me when I am expected to find pleasure through your service. You
insist that all you need is to see my pleasure. But I don't want that.

I want you.

You cry once when I take you in my mouth, half hard. I pull
away, I'm sorry. You tell me, *keep going.* I don't know. I don't
know. Why is it that much better to feel your pleasure after?

I have a studio apartment and a twin sized bed and we are filthy,
the carpet coated in dog hair the afternoon sun in the windows.
It is a disgusting animal rite better suited to teenagers than aging
bodies, our graying hair and our creaking joints. But I have

never felt so beautiful and wanted. I have never found anyone else so beautiful and worthy of want.

After that first leaving in the late summer I could not imagine ever fucking someone after you. And we see now dear reader, A., somehow I will manage. But, that autumn, I could not even cum. I would think of you sometimes and rub my thighs together or grind into the seat of a bicycle. But I could not bring myself to touch or feel without you.

I fantasized about your life with the baby those first months after his birth. The flailing hands and the hunger and hot red cheeks and the burping and the rocking. I will never know these things for myself. But I thought. In periphery. Perhaps you set the child near you and rock him with your foot while you play the piano and sing. Perhaps he makes you laugh. Perhaps some nights he makes you so afraid for the future. We talked often of ethics. I do not believe creating life, even in the best of times, is ethical. I know you must think on it still.

I ask you why she wants the baby and you say — *she just feels it is something you should do*. I cannot fathom the lack of depth to create some deep-feeling animal and thrust it into a world of suffering. To *grow* suffering in your own body just to check checks on a list of to-dos. And you love her most. You love *her* most.

And I. A sterile, jealous, vindictive and withering hag. Still here though.

I think of her with bloated ankles and sore bones and a parasite inside of her while you held my hand, and I am angry you were not more attentive to her. That I fed your inattentiveness. But you insisted she was independent. You said she was jealous, but you insisted it was manageable. Good, even. Had she not done the same to you so many times?

When I was maybe eleven my favorite book began with a woman giving birth, completely silent, so as not to demean herself. I imagine this is how your wife gives birth. Stoic and condemning of the nursing staff. Bleeding out without raising a brow. And you confirm for me later. You return to me in the winter, and you tell me about everything I have missed, pacing in my apartment, crying and vomiting and packing a bag for the hospital. A friend helping me pack, just in case I cannot take the missing anymore. While your life is flush with so much love and life and my daydreams of your full world are not so wrong.

You love her most. And so, no matter what I try, I hate her. Another unforgivable mark against me reader. Because with you A., I cannot feel anything close to hate. I try to hate you. I've tried so many times to hate you. But, I love you still so fiercely. I love you a way I did not know I could love. I forgive you everything. I cannot hate you at all, not the smallest amount. I love you now.

I love you the way you love her.

XIV

You know I've done hand stuff with your friend and you think I might fuck you. Cigar burns up your arms — you are very attractive to me. Small, intensely intelligent with a flagrant dark humor. You give me CDs. The Smiths. You give me books. Oscar Wilde. You call me every Saturday when I am usually sleeping over with friends —*if you were here I'd be making you banana pancakes.* I show them. They giggle.

Even then I was learning not to succumb to actual desire. The things you want are the things capable of inflicting real lasting wounds. Anything less ends and it is blissfully superficial. I like the affairs that say they are nothing early. Easy come.

XLIX

Every time you email me, and you email me still, as in you emailed me this morning, you inquire after my littlest hole. This is what you call it. Which I never gave you access to. Which you lament. Which you, obsess over. Which you grieve.

S. *I want. Every Both. And.* ^/* 3/2

Algebra. I always know the meaning. It is always simply anal. But you want me to solve the riddle. Understand the means. Maybe you want to remind me I am too stupid or boring to parse. My emails back must mirror the structure. It is an important part of the game.

Certainly you could have had it while I slept beside you. What useless subjective lines of morality. It amuses me. The things that are taken from me without asking, and the things that aren't. Aren't you much too clever for base human rules?

Five times today I have stood at my bathroom sink and cum to stuffed anuses. The kind of pained expression the woman makes that means she is a little bored or uncomfortable. And that is when I cum. Usually better if her pussy or mouth is crowded as well. I close the screen before the chuffed boyfriend teases the tippers, sitting on the edge of the bed, his now soft cock in his hands. Sometimes the men peacock like this when throughout the show they have done nothing more than stand to the side and observe as the woman takes a foreign object, like a large dildo or a string of oversized anal beads, and feeds herself, cheeks spread. And we all cum. And the boyfriend, often limp or struggling to raise throughout, takes the applause. The woman in the wings, tending her wounds. Her opened hole. And thinking of her tending in isolation, frowning in the mirror. This also makes me cum.

We pretend we are married.

We play journal roulette after sex, pick a date, and the dates we pick I am always going mad in Tokyo, and you are always swooning over someone or other. You were married once I think, a childhood sweetheart of some kind. Our marriage is play. But I have never lived with a lover and I think it feels like marriage. And I tell you. And you like this game and you agree to pretend with me. Each week is a year of our marriage.

You are sweet in class. You are a very good and a very kind teacher. You are quicker than some other instructors I've had but this mental dexterity does not make you any less generous to those who are slow. You listen to me talk. You like my ideas. You ask me about myself and the classes I have taken and to see my science fiction novel because you say I must be a good writer if I am such a good reader. When I send it to you, you say, *what are you so worried about. Aren't you already a writer?* And you've stolen me with that.

The moment again. You ask me out to lunch, so similar, god the repetitive nonsense, to talk about my writing. Christ, are we all just trite cliches on a loop? He left me for his wife. Another?

Again. When will you learn? It is insanity to expect them to care. It is insanity.

Writing this same scene. I am only twenty but this one year has aged me uncountably. We eat. You describe your books, the ones on your shelves. The ones you have written you will not explain to me until much later. When I read them they will shock me. I will be mad for them. I will be terrified by them. I will be made to feel incomprehensibly slow by their ambition. The smut of them will sicken me.

S. *My needs.*

S.

[...]

Do I suck your cock under your desk as you read aloud from your own filthy book? Or is this just a fantasy you have recited to me so many times I have given life to it. It hardly matters what is "real." It exists now, this memory. You have subjected me perhaps without my consent simply through your insistence, or persistence.

But sometimes I encourage you. When I am lonely. When I am sad. _____. Tell me anything?

With the first professor I was stupid and young and I think maybe we were both, dense. Clumsy. This time — you were devious. And so it is the same moment but I respect the duplicity. It makes me less a fool and so I've always hated you less. In fact. I've never hated you. Sometimes I've felt close to you, felt concern for you. And sometimes I've squirmed at the thought of you like someone finding a hair in an egg yolk. But. You knew exactly what you were doing having done it so many times before, and you did it well. And that is not so painful. To be duped by someone quite bright and quite competent at catching prey. To know every moment was a lie and we both knew it throughout also brings me quite a bit of comfort. I did know after this first moment — I did know you did not love me and this brings me pleasure.

Strangers with candy. You ask me, *Would you like to borrow a book?*

Oh, yes reader. After all I have heard of this library. I would love to borrow a book.

In your apartment, with exposed brick walls, fruit hanging from hooks, you have organized your books by geographical location. Maybe even continent, then country. Then within the category of region organized by genre. Only then is it alphabetical. And there are so many shelves. You say you reorganize them often and I say I love to do this myself. You press into my hands Fowles, who I already love, Faulkner. O'Connor. Relevant to the class you are teaching. And. I believe, many more. You give me a few authors from your home country that I do not remember the names of. I can take all of these? *Of course. I know you will appreciate them.* I will, I say.

We are seated and, I am almost sure it is chess, a small set. I am sure I was white when now I only will play black. And we are laughing. And this is how little I know of human interaction. I do not think I am flirting. I think I am laughing, engaged. Even though we have seen this goddamned exact same moment. The similarities.

Were I able to live in a year or two of quiet. Would I still have been so stupid? Would I have always been this intentionally naive whore?

When you move to kiss me I am shocked. Again. I should not

be. Again. And you may believe I have no right to be. I am too slow, too stupid.

I am also repulsed. Again. Redundantly unkind to the last.

I immediately allow this time though. Reciprocate. I know there is no out. What will I do? Pass your class after having rebuffed you? Keep the books? You are so gentle who would believe me. And even though I know what you are doing, it makes me feel so clever, so seen. I let you, continue to kiss you as your baseball cap, which you even wore in class, comes off. It is hiding that you are not the young man I thought you were. You do not have a thick head of black curls but only a few along the sides and the back and that the top of your head is not balding, but bald. Shiny.

A halo.

A joke just for me.

I imagine we probably fuck here, because I don't think I touch people without fucking them this year. I think one always comes with the other. And also, I know I move in, maybe the next week. The course you teach me is a summer course, shortened, and I live with you through most of it, taking the train in and out of the city, offering the class cupcakes I've made in your oven.

So. I should be grateful you weren't disappointed. A smarter person would have made you wait until they had somewhere to sleep. It is after the break-in, its own chapter that has nothing to do with this book. The door frame in ruins and the man with the gun, eye contact as I lay frozen on the bed — enough for here and now. Maybe I will address this man, or more likely boy, somewhere else — it is relevant only in that I have been accumulating partners so I will not have to go back. I cannot sleep in that room. I should feel very lucky I did not disappoint. Or perhaps, I only gave you one hole that night, and you were out to collect all three.

S. *My needs. I can be very demanding. That can be a good thing and a bad thing.*

Why does opening this seem, impossibly enormous, when we never loved each other. Were never anything to each other. When it was all a game we both told each other we wanted to play.

I suppose if these are all just snapshots. You took the most. The most profane. The best.

Meeting your models years later. Looking at photos of their breasts and stomachs. Their long hair. Their cut limbs. Knowing you fucked them all. The pink wig you dress me in. In the wig I am Sugar, more play. Juggling oranges in the Italian market, the key to my gym locker tied around my thick red hands.

Another aside in the narrative.

You take me to the beach. Men who are clever and who know it is the beach I really love and not any human will find a way to provide, in order to collect after. Monsters like myself. Do it early. It is an easy gambit but it makes me resent the men I care for who will not. Maybe because the men I care for do not want to be seen with me at the beach. Whole, good, real persons. They, being. And I being exposed with my scales.

We drop by Target so I can buy a cheap suit. It is a white triangle bikini with padding. It is the cheapest thing I can find and I don't have fifty cents to spare. We sit on the beach and I read Pynchon's *Crying of Lot 49* to you out loud and we write each other's names in the sand.

There is nothing in this life I love more than walking into the ocean, riding the sea when you're past the breaking waves. And you are the kind of man to be enamored with a youthful obsession. It is its own kind of aesthetic.

When we get home, your place, I called it home, we peel off our clothes to discover we are both lobster red with burns but still we manage to fuck in the shower.

But before that, on the way out we pass the mass of men. "Bros." Twenty odd and drinking beer in a crowd and every woman that passes they say yes, or no. In my felt hat, holding your arm so tightly because I am terrified of men in groups and you are all I've got. Rightfully terrified of men in groups. It is a chorus of yes for me, which is of course worse than a no, and for the first time makes me feel naked on the shore. And then they begin to mock you.

Why are you with that old man.

He has a small cock anyways.

Let me show you.

You don't know what you're missing.

You pull me closer. *What do they know.*

So maybe now is the Magnums.

I am sure we have condoms at, I will continue to call it home, because despite the artifice of the whole ordeal I wanted it to be a home. I wanted to feel safe with someone and I didn't mind if it was with you. There was so much food. There was a bed and a sofa. You would drive me to work at the Ben and Jerry's and even though I smelled like rotten milk and dead mice after my shift you would pick me up in your pretty button-up after teaching your classes and sit with me and my friend by the river and you would talk to him as thoughtfully as you talked to me and recommend him books too and we both felt so serious in your presence. I thought maybe I was home.

But you needed to buy Magnums.

I want to be clear. When I think... I know you were duplicitous, but I think in your own way you tried. And when I said it was time to end. You listened and accepted and stayed kind to me after. Not just the emails of your bulging pants and desires but also genuine inquiries into my well-being. Stories about your days. And I think you could not bear my drinking because it reminded you so of your father. Humiliating you at a bar. And in the years since I have used you for want and been unkind in return. And I think we pushed one another into — does it matter? There are many more good things, but. Considering how many of your students, younger than the twenty years that I was, climb into your bed. Does it matter?

I ask. Are you still fucking your students?

How complicit am I. Or am I enabling because I care for you still? I do not want to see you, or them, hurt. And often, I enjoyed you. I almost always responded to your touch with desire.

Standing in the CVS though, I said, do I have to go in? It was important to you that I stand in my skirt and moccasins as you bought condoms. Magnums. You asked the cashier for them.

You were bigger than many men I'd been with, yes. Your obsession.

Your thick member in my littlest hole.

I will give it to you if ever you see me again. A trade? I will give it to you. I will give you everything you want. I am just so exhausted. With myself. With all of it.

I can write this today because today I am fine. Last night I fell asleep to the video of you singing to your child A. And so what else. I slept so well.

XXXIX

You draw me anime style in lingerie and I like that you think I am pretty. Talking sometimes on our balconies, maybe once I've forgotten my key and I walk through your room to get through my sliding door. The things one grows used to in youth. Someone implies you may watch. Perhaps you witnessed my madness. I never closed the blinds.

XXXVI

My two male friends engaged in conversation with two younger women and I am sitting alone at the bar and an older man, clearly wealthy, slips his hand on my leg and up my thigh. I just sit there like that, pretending nothing is happening at all, until either he walks away or the boys rejoin me and frighten him off.

XXXII

During the Mikoshi festival I am quite thin and unwell carrying the shrine and drinking beer instead of water every break does not help. It is mostly men. I am given the opportunity when the sun has set to carry a lantern. I accept. A man grabs me under the soft light, kisses me full on the mouth. Laughter. *A beautiful woman,* someone translates, *how could he not.*

That night we finally eat. And drink. And karaoke. But over the soup I use the word umai which I have read. Deeply satisfying. Delicious. The men. My three young male American friends, our older Japanese companions, laugh at me again. The education continues. A woman's voice, *oishi,* a man's voice, *umai.* Over and over.

Okay. I remember what I am. My holes my identification and my use.

LII

You want me so much. I crinkle my nose. Disdainful. I must
have believed, I must still in part believe, that I was, or am. The
only bad woman. The only woman foul enough to want the
flesh. When my partners are wet for me there is always this
moment of revulsion. You should not want. A deep belief in me
I cannot overwrite. A woman should not want.

But to myself — you are not a woman, you are something worse.

You kiss me at my windowsill and push against me almost
mounting my thigh and I say, no. No, you're too young. But still
we kiss. You sleep in my bed. We paint one large canvas
together in my living room. Your side is beautiful and perfect, a
portrait, mine is something like the gates of hell. Cartoonish.
Smeared. I take you to parties and feel pleasure at your beauty
and standing near your arm in a kitchen of my peers saying, this
is my girlfriend. I'm twenty-two and you're eighteen and we've
been seeing each other since the first kiss. A basement show but
we've spent the night on the roof talking about despair and the
stars and when we return to the concert I push you against a

wall and kiss you. And you do not only accept this, but kiss me back, hard.

You tell me you're going to art school out of state. It is only on our third or fourth date that you reveal, no. You go to High School. The filth of me now rebounded and turned against someone I care for. I am ashamed that I should enact these old patterns from the other side. I say. I can only see you as a friend. Maybe when you're eighteen. Or maybe I say. We can date but nothing physical. But you are so beautiful it is agony. With your long red hair and skinny legs. I just like being seen with you. Your thoughts are young in that they are sad in a way you think is boundless when I know you have just begun to discover a life-time of sadnesses. I know that as they copulate they will sway as they stack. But I cannot explain that to you and it is a burden.

You take a polaroid of me before I go to inpatient. Not at my worst yet but still my arms are bones in the photo and though it is a beautiful July day I ask if we can sit down in the shade. You visit me while I am in too. You bring me a flower you have blown out of glass and I show it to my therapist and he says, *this is the first time I've seen you happy like this*. I tell him. But, she is too young.

When you are older you visit and perhaps sleep on my futon with me and still I cannot find the courage. I take a polaroid of you before you leave. Black and white in your new masculine clothes. Missing that I cannot find a way over to you. Beneath the photo you took of me that July day, you ask me for my LGBTQ narrative, my coming out story. It is a project. You hand me a sharpie. I write in the white margin — HOW?

LXXX

We've been fucking for months but when I try to introduce you to friends I find I can't force the shape of your name into my mouth. Not even the first letter.

XVII

Sometimes during sex you hold both my ankles above my head with one hand and the shame I feel when you do this it caught still in my throat like a gag. It reminds me of changing a diaper. To be seen in this position. To have a sweating man inside of a place I have not yet found the courage to explore and treating it, me, like he is changing a shit filled diaper. To be infantilized. The loss of control. I like it best from behind still. I like not to see the indignity of what is being done to me. Allowed to feel pleasure without witnessing my debasement. I still hate to shave completely the way you liked it. To be exposed and vulnerable. Closeness. Vulnerability. Care. That is not what I bring to sex or historically what I look to it for.

One very notable exception to this rule.

A. Are you still reading? A. Are you bored and will you leave me again here to face the rest alone?

So needy, they complain of me. *You ask too much.*

I ask strangers frequently, but what is the role of porn? I wonder if this is human nature, the shifting from position to position callously, without speaking to the woman, or in this case, adolescent. Moving their body in ways that they may have never imagined they could be moved. I did not watch porn when I was young and many of the shapes my body was forced into confounded me. The imagination of my partners, who were in fact using me as a dummy, a facsimile of what they had visually consumed and enjoyed. Many of these cocks are not cocks I fucked, or rarely fucked, but were instead cocks masturbating inside my body. While I thought about the weather, the shape of my stomach, or while I tried to tolerate it longer and longer and better and better. Prettier and prettier.

A recent hook up, otherwise absent from these pages. *If only you could see this. This looks so fucking hot.* Good. In my old age I've finally mastered being a shape. He keeps one leg up, not realizing it is merely a pose for the benefit of the camera, not me.

You were, persistent. My memory is not good enough to know and I'm sure I wanted it often. I grew attached to you too. I'm not always sure how much I liked you though. Driving without hands on winding roads. The thick combat boots with the smiley face on the toe. The first time we made out watching *Donnie Darko* in your parent's house. This too. When my boyfriend before you would ask me for certain things, I would say no. I wonder now. Was it because he was my age? Poor like me in a one-bedroom apartment? I wonder, was it because he was Black? You are a few years older than me and go to a different high school. You are the richest member of our group of friends. White and your parents have spoiled you. I cannot help but wonder what, how much, any of that means. What gears were turning in my subconscious that made me submit to you when I did not to others.

The sex often felt like a humiliation. I do not know if it was only because I was young. I imagine sex is for many people, nothing more than a humiliation. You also pushed often for things I did not want to offer. You were also politically correct and feminist and progressive. And, as was mentioned, well off. I always assumed you knew best, or at least better, than I. You were obsessed with making me cum. In fact I think many of the things tried were attempted to accommodate this obsession. There were a few times I remember... I remember, and it might not be true, saying no and pushing you away. And you returning hungry.

The day in the park in particular. I am sure this day I said no at least once. Fucking me over a bench so several people on the trail saw. The condom breaking. I remember shivering and crying in the passenger seat of your car drawing my knees to my chest talking rapidly and willing the sperm to fall out of me, waiting for your friend's older sister to come and buy us the Plan B. For hours. Long hours in the parking lot moving the car every so often in case someone would ask us to leave. Terrified of having your child, for it to have been conceived like this. Terrified of becoming my mother. And you did not understand the worry. In your left leaning world perhaps you thought it would be as simple as an abortion. You were used to these things. I would have seen it as a cruel kind of fate though, a sign from God, and would have followed through with resignation. To birth myself. I was sixteen.

Maybe it was the car I loved. Not just fucking half out of the backseat or straddling you while you were at the wheel but the places it could take me. Anything was a fair payment to be away.

When I was sick with mono, I could barely swallow. I could barely keep my eyes open. As ill as I've ever been but sitting in your car still I would beg you no, please don't take me back yet. Please let me stay here a little longer. And you acquiesced.

Playing guitar at a party, letting me put a yellow flower behind your ear. The metro in DC. Checking my makeup in your car's mirror before kissing you and you complaining, *why are you so vain*. Fucking me in the light of the moon so Diana could see me better.

Your friend driving to my house, _____ *needs you*. I don't even have my permit yet. You are so drunk you are non-syllabic. You are cut from broken glass and I tend to you, put you in the car with your friend's help before the cleaning ladies arrive, drive you to a parking lot somewhere and sit with you, waiting. After the hours of anxiety, the cops circling the lot, depositing you back into the care of your friend. You terrify me but I like doing this thing for you. I like to do things for my lovers which is maybe why I ask too much. I am hoping they will ask me too. I can help. I can accommodate so much.

When I tell you anal is too painful, it is grueling for me. I never complain during sex. I can think of two other times. Bent over your parent's bed, no lube, and I can see myself in the mirror and the humiliation is, unspeakable. Nothing has ever been inside this orifice except perhaps an enema as a child. My cheeks are red with pain and I am still in a t-shirt. Maybe my hands behind my back, maybe tied, and I feel dirty and afraid. I ask you, please stop. You say you are almost finished. And this moment must be so common. Too common to count. You use this trick often. *Do you know how painful blue balls are? You would not want to hurt me like that would you?* I say, I can't, please. I believe I say please. I believe I ask three times. You pull yourself out of my ass and without telling me what you are doing — or maybe you do and I nod or in some other way assent, I don't know, but it shocks me still — without changing the condom, you fuck my cunt until you cum. When I go to the bathroom after my vagina is full of fecal matter and I cannot clean up that far with my fingers, with soap it stings. I shit relentlessly and after, mucous, bloody. Something is torn. I feel the filth of my body. I am the filth. I am nothing more than the filth. I cannot look at my own hands.

Leaving the bathroom when I have done all I can.

XL

It is when I've returned from Turkey, running an Airbnb for somewhere to live. I invite you over. We are maybe drinking, talking, in the living room. Maybe I ask you to fuck. Maybe we are already on the floor. You push your cock into my mouth and throat with my back on the linoleum floor, a form of penetration I have not allowed you previously. I am wide eyed and slack as it happens. I respond to aggression with compliance. When you are finished you stand. A guest opens the door and we jerk apart.

You tell me you should apologize later, *You asked me not to leave after. I left.* I say, oh. I had forgotten but I remember now. Yes, I did not like that. Yes. That scared me.

We meet in undergrad and play like the children we are. I find it exhilarating to act my age again after dating the first professor. At a show in my basement you are intrigued not irritated by my excited run of sentences. You are tall with a wry sarcastic wit that strikes me often as more cruel than intelligent. We smoke weed in your dorm room and play video games and watch *Antichrist* and *A Scanner Darkly*. We drink forties at ___

House, half listening to the bands, and you drop your phone in the toilet trimming your pubes for our date. You have three roommates and sometimes when you want me you will selfishly lock them all out.

These last two are interesting because of the common flavor of them. The crimes committed in what should be a healthy dynamic. Not crimes — offenses. So normal.

Questioning again. Maybe this is what the text is for. Not narrative. Not your attention A., your comprehension or pity. Maybe I simply want an exorcism. I want to be finished with this project and made glittering steel. I want to be baptized in the filth of it all, even these small perfectly normal bits of refuse — submerged beneath a thick molasses tub of all the indignities — and pulled forth. Spotless. Hairless. Without weight or holes. Newly impenetrable and lovable. Capable of love. Royal.

Or, is this stupid book merely a re-traumatization. They are truly lacerations each one.

A student this week — in an excited flurry of words that leaves his classmates looking away from their screens, uncomfortably scratching their noses and drumming their fingers — leads the class from the Vietnam War to *Toy Story* to his own personal traumas to Sontag to a bad year for an essayist in 2006 and towards the end exclaims with passion — *What if some art SHOULD just exist because PAIN exists. What if some art SHOULD just document the pain!?*

I rebuke. Certainly not. Who disagrees with ___ here? Who will disagree on my behalf, as I cannot. I can see the way I am allowed to seep into their minds despite my best intentions to keep them pure. How to educate without dirtying.

And you too are seduced by a professor. Comparing notes. You are all ethics now. All standards. One mistake so long ago when I have accrued so many more than you. When you needed kindness and I kept aloof. When you told me you were a person, and I looked, confused. You too, have needs?

What does it matter. Why am I writing. Reader? A.? Why not just a small note of concession to your love. Why something so tired and long?

XIX

Each of these that feign isolation we have already proven work instead towards an irrefutable group effect. I still take my coffee black to impress you. You are in your twenties? Maybe just twenty? I am sixteen. You buy me coffee. You are a construction worker and "manly" and so of course drink yours without milk or sugar but I have only had caramel macchiatos at the mall a few times with friends and you are sick of paying for them, so you start ordering me hot chocolate. I cannot bear for you to make me a child though. I want your body. Drinking vodka on your bed in your parent's house and we take turns massaging each other until I think I will die from the want. *Not here.* You take me outside. Remove my tampon for me, put it in your pocket? We both smoke, I think even while we fuck. And I have burns on the top of my breasts from the ash as you thrust.

Sitting in your barn afterwards I put my legs over you under a quilt, the summer nights cooling. We talk about death. We talk about wanting death. We want death relentlessly, more than we want sex. Barely, but more.

I meet you at a party in the summer, maybe a week after I have moved to Pennsylvania. Smoking together on the balcony with the Christmas lights twinkling and the shouting inside of beer pong and delight. I almost forgot. You gave me my Plath. My unabridged diaries. Thank you so much. You were always careful with me. Thank you for that too.

I am grateful for all of you who were, compassionate, who did not believe me when I insisted I did not need soft handling. Who knew better and bought me hot cocoas.

You are the same class as me. I know this. I don't know it consciously but I know when I leave you it is for upward mobility.

Your younger sister has nightmares so loud she screams. You cook for me in your mother's kitchen and tell me, confidingly, *she does not want to be associated with us.* The big Irish Catholic family and the smell of, your, my, our social place. A thousand meals, each of them lingering somehow in the air. Open windows. I think. Why am I choosing this? Just for a body?

I cannot remember the details of your trauma I am sorry. It was so long ago and I was so absorbed in my own pain. I remember letting you cry. I remember the importance of being understood. And of course, I remember the vodka.

We go to Philly and you show me South Street for the first time and teach me how to fold my pizza and we visit the Magic Garden and I am sure I have never seen anything so beautiful. We drink rum in your cousin's apartment and you push me against the walls with want. I want too, so much. We maybe think we can replace the want for death with a want for each other.

Why could I not have been as gentle with you as you were with me? Again, the repetitive nature of that question, I'm sorry reader as I see this is all growing redundant, but, I truly did not believe he could care.

You were older. I did not leave you well, I'm sorry. I was punished for it though. Is this a justice you seek? I am the school slut within my first month. Girls I sat with at lunch the first week refusing me a space. Everything from twittering behind my back to open confrontation. It actually feels like nothing to me. I have experienced it all before.

I will see arches in the city even now and think of you driving me through places you'd built. *This. With my hands. I did this.* So proud. Those hands that built those things, inside me.

I would clip your hair with scissors.

I am so far away now from being able to clip someone's hair in the living room. Who would trust me with something so delicate.

LVII

One night I go with _____ , reader, you will meet him later, to
see a play. Sam Shepard, *The Curse of the Starving Class*.
When I go to his shows he always reserves the same seat for me,
my favorite, in the third row on the left hand side of the theatre
one seat away from the aisle so I can see the entire stage, but
also, spy on him in the wings. This play we sit together,
somewhere near the back.

After the show he wants me to come home with him, but I have
been changed. I have been awakened. I have seen myself in the
naked body eating butter onstage. I cannot pretend tonight to be
anything but the dirt I am.

Weston: My poison scares you.
Wesley: Doesn't scare me.
Weston: No?
Wesley: No.
Weston: Good. You're growing up. I never saw my old man's
poison until I was much older than you. Much older. And then
you know how I recognized it?
Wesley: How?

Weston: Because I saw myself infected with it. That's how. I saw me carrying it around. His poison in my body.

We have fucked maybe once before after months of flirtation and meaningful conversations and it did not go the way we had hoped. I would stand behind the front desk at the high-end gym where I was working. I had night shifts and there were few people coming in or out so I would read. You would walk over from the juice bar and fold your arms and lean over the desk. *What have you got there?*

There are other men from this gym, all of a different class from me though, and so the bond was not there. I actually cannot imagine a better setting for a romance based on poverty than here, with the executive keys, celebrities, the Mayor popping by. My pristine blue collared shirt and brown eyeshadow. Maybe the only other person who understood me as much as you, some executive. But I think he'd grown up poor in North Philly. A boxer. He would also talk to me in the nights. I quite liked him. Defensive when other men wanted my attention though. *Is he bothering you?* No. Yes, and no. It is always so difficult for me to see the difference between kindness and something more. The boxer related most to Jon Snow in *Game of Thrones*. When he heard I did not have a television he brought one in his car for me. *Let me drive you home I can install it.* And how did I manage to say no to that one while still remaining in his employ? Look, each year we see how much smarter I am becoming. Or, how much more cynical. Perhaps he was only being generous. Fatherly. And the forever doubt is as difficult as anything else.

I have a crush. A film buff who loves comics and Tom Robbins. Very tall with a wide face and big grin, a gap between the front teeth. This is when I had begun to actively and consciously restrict and you made me smoothies to my specific qualifications. My skin already marked with the yellow sheen of jaundice that would grow worse and worse through the summer.

I am in love with _____, but after the play, I know I cannot be with him. I wept throughout the Shepard and as we left he did not understand. He did not and would never know. We walk past a billboard of his sculpted thighs on the way out of the theater.

After the play I rush home to change. I put on lipstick and perfume and a lingerie slip I still have from that first affair. It is cold but the only thing I put over it is my coat. I pack my back-pack with flour and sugar and baking soda. My roommates. *What are you doing?* Distress and unbridled need that creates its own kind of energy. I bike from almost one end of the city to the other. My bare cunt under the slip barely covered by the coat.

When I arrive at your place I knock on the door. I don't even know if I've called ahead and I know you have a girlfriend but you are alone and as soon as you close the door behind you I am on my knees. I have never given a more urgent blow job in my life, I will die if you do not make me who I am. I must be on my knees. You must push against the back of my head and you must make me what I am. After you cum and I swallow, before we even speak to one another, I move to the kitchen.

I tell you. I need to bake you bread.

I bake. I do not have a recipe I am just pouring ingredients into a bowl. You fuck me half in the oven, probably. Probably at my request. While I bake I am bent over counters and against book-shelves. My hands on the floor. I find honey in your otherwise bare cupboards and pour it into the batter. It is full of black ants but it doesn't matter. I like the way they look drowned in some-thing so sweet. Pretty and still and I want them inside of me too.

I am sure I cannot tell you what came out of the oven that night, but our affair begins and it is a great comfort for us both I believe to be ourselves. To be the products of the backgrounds we otherwise pretend we have outgrown. But it is also turmoil. Shame. Enabling our worst parts.

Your favorite film is, *They Shoot Horses, Don't They?* And we are so beaten. Together we can admit we are so beaten. The night you come home after seeing your father and you scream, not at me but at whatever made us this way — furious with hurting — and fall face forward flat on your mattress your feet hanging off the bed, blacked out from whiskey. I believe I unlace and remove your shoes for you. Check to see if you are breathing.

But, I am ahead of myself.

It is before I have moved into your attic. A night when I have come over to sit on your floor — you insist I can have a chair or the bed, but I tell you I much prefer the floor and it is true — and we watch films. Sometimes you will let me show you something but you have so much you want to share. We drink. This is when I begin drinking beer, before mostly wine or vodka, and ever since, an important part of my person. A beer here in the afternoon to still the nerves. To feed, remembering you.

You encouraged my vain obsession with my weight. When I eventually became so thin you can not only feel but see the organ of my heart beating. Slowly. The bradycardia already inching. And in a way that made the first nurse who saw my nude chest audibly gasp so I squirmed with pleasure. You let me lean back, arched over your forearms — thick like a working man's should be, you would say — and you would put your hand, half the size of my torso, just beneath my left breast and over the beating organ. Holding it. Because sometimes I was sure it would pulse its way out of my body. And you didn't want me to worry about losing it.

You're the one who convinces me to leave my job. *You could write*, you say, *if you had more time.* I am going to school during the day and working at the gym and also at Barnes and Nobles and Urban Outfitters. I have mostly stopped eating anything but jam in lettuce leaves, canned peas, the smoothies you make me, beer. I lack the ability to sleep, as do you, without blacking out. So we sit in a lit room through the night, and tremble, and share.

One night you are getting angry. Very angry and giving me memories from your childhood. I am backing away but I have backed away as far as I can and so now I am very calm because I have seen men agitated like this and I am very calm and I sit against the wall while you punch around my head. And there are holes in the drywall. Close to my jaw.

You were just angry, there's nothing else to say about it.

You tell me, *so you don't have to work. Why don't you live in my attic? I won't charge you rent.*

I remember broken glass. Besides the ants in the honey there were other small indignities that we, two people who liked to soak in our decrepitness, encountered. There was the time I was cooking in your kitchen — borscht, we had just finished rereading *Jitterbug Perfume* and I was on a beet diet — when your girlfriend, who had broken up with you, came to collect her belongings. My mind was so foggy with hunger I don't remember everything. I stood near you. A ways off. She looked at me. She, an upper middle-class woman with wide hips over six foot. I am maybe a third of either of you. She does not acknowledge or speak to me but turns red in the cheeks and spits, if not literally, in spirit.

_____. *She is tiny.*

You tell me, *maybe it would be a good idea to take a walk.*

I walk around the block. Too tired and too stupid to have any thoughts at all. When I return I see your girlfriend has thrown something through your window, or perhaps just pushed your air conditioning unit out onto the street. Glass everywhere. And something in this memory seems false, the timeline or the events. But also it is a memory that is there, that I believe is grounded in truth. I remember plastic covering the window.

I perhaps do not even comment on it but fall asleep, either in your bed or mine. Regardless of the place I think you hold me while I would sleep often. You tell me I am beautiful and you will make sure I am safe. You worry you say, *it seems you have the weight of the world.* I argue I have only the smallest things. Everything is so small.

There was always beer in the fridge.

You were working, still at the juice bar, when I moved in. You had bought me some of my favorite things though and they were waiting for me. Stouts. IPAs. Belgian Triples.

The room in the attic was my first real space. It was big and I found a free table to set up as a desk. You gave me bookshelves. I had a mattress and lamps. My own bathroom. When you came home from work that first day I was moved and sitting on the porch in short shorts drinking and painting a nude. A four foot canvas filled with a beautiful fat woman. She hangs behind me in the pictures I will take to document my weight loss. _____, _____. _____. The numbers my favorite, cemented in my memory but I will not give them what they want. I will not allow myself the pleasure of writing them here.

I wanted more and smaller, and my heart would not let me see the number I most desired.

During this period I would write. You would encourage me to write.

We would sit in our respective rooms, you watching films or playing video games. Me. Writing. Writing writing writing writing. I would rush down the stairs to read aloud to you a poem.

You took care of me sometimes. But, I believe I was too ill then for you to fuck. Just bones and everything hurt.

I would listen to you fuck other women in the room beneath me. Like a wraith creeping up and down the stairs for a cold beer, the warmth of the only other room in the house, the two bodies inside. I did not want the women to see me. Skeletal and a color wrong for flesh. Otherwise, just writing. Poems and novels and incomprehensible trash. One night an old friend who has an internship in NYC visits me. We all go to a club. You fuck her after and I listen to that too. But you never say you will kick me out. You still listen to my poems when I stand in your doorway and recite them to you.

Your big hands still hold my arms and face after the nightmares.

When I am institutionalized you still allow me to keep my things in your attic.

Two months after leaving, after I am sedated with drugs and bloated with force feeding, I move my things out again. You are not there. I throw away the painting. There is never any resolution. How would I ever contact you to ask where we went? What was me. I don't even remember your full name.

LXIV

I interrogate if I am getting off on these, enjoying replaying the memories, especially the bad ones. Perhaps a little. A little addicted to licking at my own wounds. But so many I have not revisited for so long it is a bit of an adventure. A discovery.

Perhaps.

The novel you send me, "about" me. The brothel where I whisper in your ear. My naked body on your bed growing younger and younger. The scene you write where I am sleeping and am passed around a circle of men, used. When I come to you, you partake, tears obstructing your sordid lust.

I have cum to this too.

So I am not above believing you if you think I am enjoying this. I am not above trusting your better and more intelligent observations.

In your book it turns out I was dead all along.

Wouldn't that be nice?

Instead of the author, shouldn't we kill the muse? Give them some rest.

XXIV

And in the story *you* write — it is funny the way men despise
memoir, call it cheap and easy but write stories that are simply
their lives under the guise of fiction, taking credit for the actions
of others... as if you invented my madness and I did not carry it
into your kitchen — I am crying. My head is out the window so I
can smoke and cry while you fuck me. I stop you before you
finish. I ask you to play the same Jeff Buckley song, we know
which, over and over and over and over and over. I finish crying.
I sit down and I drink a Corona.

My interiority insignificant. What, reader, was I thinking with
my torso half out that third floor window?

It is not a question the story cares much for.

Your poems are about your own pain in childhood. The acid.
You still have a girlfriend when you take me back to watch
Woody Allen on your futon. I write you a note in lipstick on
your mirror when I leave before you wake. I want to fuck on the
floor, *but my knees*, you insist. It is eternally irritating to me, the

pain I endure for men's pleasure. When they complain to me about their knees, or their backs, or their fingers.

If I complained we would get nothing done.

XXII

You are the first person I fuck after _____ leaves me and I think.
I remember now. This is what it is like to be with a man. Tall
and blonde and muscled.

I tell you I am on my period and you don't care. You fuck me
every other hour through the night and I bleed all over your
sheets. You live in Chinatown and we drink cheap cocktails at
the restaurant under your apartment.

My roommate laughs at me as I preen before going to see a show
alone on campus. What are you getting dressed up for? *Do you
think some handsome single man is going to, sit next to you, give
you his number, and ask you to coffee?*

I can feel you breathing on my neck from the seat behind me.

LXX

You I treated so poorly. Volatile. And you knew the whole time it was wrong. Shakshuka on the roof. A blindfold during sex. My red dress, hoping to die on my motorbike, taking the turns too suddenly. Not thinking of how you would have been forced to watch. Lily and the Jack of Hearts. A final breakfast of bún riêu.

Years later in Chicago, even though you are smart enough not to kiss me, deigning to take one of my paintings. Kind enough to say you found it fine.

LXXXII

I have to go pick up my youngest.

The twelve year old who of all your children is the most difficult because he is too much like you.

Then.

Kiss me.

Not after that, I beg. Not like this. And you hold my shoulders and kiss me anyways. And I leave the car and walk up the stairs. I want to be a different person who doesn't think it is worth anything for the preceding moment — the moment when you look at me and say, *you're so smart and good I'm so proud of you.* You let me bury my face in your arm and hold it with all of my strength and just sit like that. Until, of course, you need to pick up your true child. Children. Your sports car in the rain. I've seen many of them. They are all the same bright color. Your favorite.

I wonder if I had been a different person, if I would have known there was a violent rot at the center of your interests. After the first time you take me out to dinner, maybe I could have stopped it then? I have been working in the office with you for maybe six months, in your bars for maybe a year. You hire me because you want me I can tell. The rest of your staff can tell too. I don't mind though as long as I get the job. And in the office there is a frequency. You hover around me. You tease me too much but also it is a gentler ribbing than the way you will lash out suddenly with others. One day we are both hunting for something in a closet and you just look into my eyes, and I hold the look.

The morning after the first night you sit me in front of your desk. You are in your chair behind it, the door cracked for others in the office, and you speak softly although it must look as though I am about to be disciplined. I am so ashamed I can barely keep my head up. The night before after negronis on an empty stomach. I am so nervous and you order more for me saying I am such a pleasure like this. You say you have never seen someone so changed after a drink. I slide my hands up your thigh. I instigate. You follow through. You bring me back to the office and I take off my top. Straddle you. You put your hands around my naked back. And you wanted to be held as much as I did. Needed to be held. And then vomiting on your office floor. You, driving me home. The next day I am late to work and so you take me to your office for chastisement. Sitting in front of you at your desk. What do we even say to one another. Do I say anything at all?

You tell me I should look more hungover I think. And I am pleased.

The affair after.

Mostly you running your hands up my legs, maybe a finger inside. Mostly in your office. Drinks at bars where no one will know you. Spots for college bros. Once, a night sitting on my futon watching you play guitar above me. Closing down a restaurant as I order everything off the menu, one entrée after the other. The day I leave you say you just want to be alone with me. You offer to pay for a hotel, but the one across the street is the same one where I spent nights with the first professor. I tell you it is tainted. This last day we are at the office but you feign an errand and you sit me in your car and hold my hand and give me a gift. A shirt I compliment every time you wear it. A good pen in a felt lined box. You promised me I would like the gift and I do. Calling you one night years later, looking for comfort, locked out of _____'s, sleeping in my car. And you give me the love I need willingly. Patiently, despite every-thing else in your world.

No one could ever make me feel so special.

The first time I see you when I've returned to Philadelphia from Chicago. I have four cocktails alone while you yell, maybe at your lawyer, on the phone. The bartender attentive to me. The cocktails maybe the most expensive on the menu, you'll pay. I remember this too. You always make time for me but you are always in the midst of a crisis. *It seems fair Sam, that you should return on what is maybe the worst day of my life.* And when you're off the phone — after shots of local whiskey you cry about your father. A long story. You want to know you are a good son to both your parents. I hug you. Touch the tears on your cheek. It is odd that I believe it is true we missed each other. Whatever this is, I don't think you can say there is nothing real here. You tell me you love me, and whether you actually do or not, I love you. I actually do. How else could it hurt so much.

I'm sitting in your car because I feel safe in your car when you hurt me. And, as I said, you make me special, you make me matter. When you must hurt other women too. On our date, talking about your new office assistant, the way she looks in your eyes and understands you. I'm not quite thirty and you're nearing sixty. Still. I've aged beyond your interest.

Taking off my clothes you look at my body like it is a thing. *You could still be twenty you know.*

I run into two of your former employees at a coffee shop. They're talking about you. Dark whispers.

I have a dream. You are driving me somewhere in your blue car, somewhere along a coast in Japan. The waves roll huge and full and cartoonish. We watch as the car in front of us drives into the swirling ocean. Is swallowed. We watch the man drown. Calm.

In the dream we arrive at a small house with green furniture. Pastel mossy green. You leave me there.

What is empathy good for, especially selected.

When we open up this last conversation you begin by regaling me with the history of the block, the building, the bar. You are an expert on the 1980s, before I was born. I listen politely. I laugh. I sit on your right side so you will have a better view of my best angle. When you start touching me I let you.

My manager at your bar would goad me. *Are you "friends" with* _____? I said yes. _____ and I are friends.

One of the women on your soccer team A. Another former coworker. When you tell her you are dating me.

They were fucking the boss, everyone knew it. In front of you and the entire team.

When I wasn't, not yet. But somehow it was predetermined. I stink of sin and because of this stink I deserve small humiliations. I deserve to be outed for my desires, for who I am desired by. I deserve to be kept quarantined, a red letter, a sign slung around my neck — or is just the scent of me enough? Some loves are bad, yes. But, perhaps lying about them, covering them up, does not help address the problem.

I have to go pick up my youngest.

III

A.

It is funny this thing I want so much should be such a vile memory.

We spend the day together and your wife is throwing a New Years party and I pout and you invite me. I should not have taken you up on your offer. I should have been wiser. But isolation has warped me. I would like so much not to be alone again. I would like so much to be in proximity to *you,* who I love. To be in proximity to someone I love when the year changes into something new, like it is an omen that the year will be full of joy, closeness.

It is a different omen. Or perhaps just a lesson. You and your wife are both teachers after all. A lesson in place.

I have no money and nothing to wear, I have sold all my good clothes throughout the year for food money, booze money. I find a five dollar black top at a store much too young for me. I cannot afford contacts so I am in big round glasses and my skin is blistered with old scars from the acne that has plagued me throughout unemployment. Coated in makeup. Not only do I not look beautiful, I don't even look good. Sickly. Poor. I wonder every day if I had been more beautiful, if I had been more stable with my own home I could invite you to, serving you and your wife cocktails. If I had been less desperate and sniveling, if then you would have wanted me. You say it doesn't matter. That no form or shape of me would have been good enough to have a place in your life. But still, I wonder.

You open the door and you are magnificent. Your wife, always when I arrive she manages to be walking down the stairs like an heiress. Her fully silver hair and the glow of her perfect complexion. Thin fingered hands soft, but now I know, with dirt beneath the nails. A secret juxtaposition to her manicured black pantsuit. Was I hoping she would have a visible paunch? Was I hoping she would be worn from the pregnancy, not full and glowing? Yes. Absolutely. I am hoping she will be ugly and drained.

I did not hate her before you left me the first time. I swear. I did not understand her, and I did not like the way she treated me, but I did not hate her. After the first leaving though. Then I allowed myself bitterness. Jealousy. Condemnation. She hugs me. I hate to be hugged — which you know — but my wants are not something to bother with here. Here I am meeting the woman who has controlled my life for the past year. I must be grateful in her presence. I must be grateful for whatever she allows, whatever gestures she may make to acknowledge my personhood. I have not seen her since the first leaving in the summer when she was still pregnant.

She tells me, *welcome*. I tell her. I love your son. I think it probably was the wrong choice.

The kitchen and dining room are full of mostly men. Maybe twenty guests of mostly men my own age but of a different sort. Boring. Rich. Eating and drinking slowly and discussing politics on a granular level. Speaking for the masses who are too stupid to comprehend what they do on their behalf. I sit with the dogs and marvel at the buffet. This year has stolen all the confidence I had begun to accumulate in graduate school and puts me back in my place. Not just you A., but sometimes being with you is a humiliation. I look so young and your pregnant wife at home and they must guess the thing that I offer you. But it is also the relentless humiliation of the job hunt. It is also the taxation of a solitude that seems, not temporary, but my fixed state. The lonely twin bed.

A man approaches, asks me how I have come to be at the party. This is his first question as I am a clear outlier. Wide-eyed. I just look at you across the room and say, I know A. We begin a polite conversation. You join us, *Sam is a fiction writer*, said with authority as if I am a fiction writer and not just an unpublished nothing. _____ *is a poet*. The man. *How do you know each other?* I, blush. I don't want to embarrass you I don't know what to say. I am a fan. I concoct a narrative in which I reach out after reading your New Yorker story, what a bizarre lie. The man forced to awkwardly step around it. And the conversation rolls forward, a little bit of writing, a little bit of politics, a turn, perhaps because I am present, I don't know how much I control these things, eventually, to porn. First the glamour of seventies porn, the production value. Then. And it is not me who instigates. Chaturbate. Cam girls. While I view these sites as something bordering on extortion, this poet views them as a wild frontier of egalitarian want. He believes it to be all consensual all willing. I try not to laugh at him. But what would sex look like in a utopia? Without power. Would it look like play?

A., you are making me another cocktail and we are discussing the difference between playing and fucking. You meet my eye. I do not think I imagine it. I would wager a third distinction now. I would raise a third and necessary point.

We are interrupted, perhaps you are needed, perhaps you check on the baby upstairs. Someone has baked cookies and when your wife sees attendees eating them she puts them aside, scolding her own guests, *for later*. I meet the eyes of the guilty party who looks at me forlorn. I mouth despite myself, *you're fine,* and when her back is turned he takes another. Undermining her perfect authority, I'm giddy.

I attach myself to a large man with a thick handlebar mustache who is less refined and dull than the rest of the party, quite funny and loud and happy to listen to my trivial banter. He fetches me food and drink so I don't have to embarrass myself by moving. I am seated in the center of the kitchen so I can see you perfectly A. anywhere you travel, a woman once joining our conversation. As she explains her important work, a lawyer of some kind, I am watching your face over her shoulder. Lit and engaged and the room is charmed around you. Your wife the flint and steel both making way for you, the spark. And I understand your marriage better if still not fully. And you sit next to me outside near the fire, offer me your coat. A woman watches us and frowns. I do not know if I should try to speak to her but ultimately decide I am too far fallen in her eyes already. Nowhere to go but down.

Landslide at midnight. But it seems too on point and I embarrass myself asking you not to. Not asking. Shrill over the music, please it is too sad.

The same woman who watched us through the fire mocks me at the end of the night. I say I was a Boy Scout. I don't know why I say this. She looks at me, up and down, *you?* I try to explain the logic of the statement, the complexity of Mormon summer camps, my relationship with my father, and then think better of it. The fire is climbing and despite all of the progressive rhetoric, you A. are the man — the men around the fire tending and fixing — the women happily standing off a bit and sick of me standing with them, but not allowing me any closer to the flames. Your wife who is your wife and this is your home. And it is so big and I feel so small and stupid and I am tired of being too much and too strange and always less than. Always other. And I walk home, my long coat against the dark.

XXXV

Isn't he a little "rapey," someone in the dorms said he was. I say,
oh yes, I will support her. But I am used to this kind of behavior
in my own room. Mostly I can weasel my way out or acquiesce
so it feels like a decision I'm making. Sometimes not. You are
obsessed with me. You steal my expensive mustard sweater just
to smell it. Everyone knows you're the only one I won't take
inside me and you can't bear it.

Years later you send me a painting you've done of me. I do not
praise it and you are quick to anger. You tell me, *other people say
it's great.*

I see myself here. I see how we are similarly disgusting.

*A., A., A. Others say you owe me, something. Look at me A., tell
me you are sorry. Take it away. Please, A., please.*

But, Christ. What a grotesque thing you are. Sweating red.

LIII

The second time we meet for drinks I greet the doorman. I have grown used to doormen this year. I take the elevator up to your floor where you meet me. Another funny man. Doing a bit. I am nicer when I am younger so I pretend to laugh. Your apartment is an enormous two bedroom in Center City with wrap-around windows and I can see the city lit with winter light and snow. Gasping. I told you I like beer, I must already be seeing _____ , regulating one side of the spectrum with the other, and you have bought several bottles of one of my favorites. We sit on your sofa and with the snow and the beer we talk. I am surprised you thought I would care that you are short. But I recognize it is a deeply ingrained thing. I remember the tall heeled cowboy boots you wear to and from the gym. You have a huge television and I cannot help myself, I beg, can we watch some? The true object of my affection.

We find a film that for me is a pulsing joy. I begin to act it out for you, tell you what is coming before it arrives. It is just our second date but I am so giddy from the pirates and the pleasure of the snow and the beer I straddle you and you take me to bed and I ride you — the expression on your face beneath me, I feel so satisfied, is one of awe. When I wake the next morning the snowy winter light, you say, *you are beautiful like a picture*. This favorite line again. Validation to remain existent.

LIV

How did these men approach me? Standing at my desk and
reading my books. Fetching them their locker keys and fixing my
lipstick. How many of you throughout the course of a first
evening would thoroughly admit to just feeling owed. After
your promotion, or your new company. After your divorce.
After too many years alone. That I would exist for you from the
gods or whatever it was that was there to provide. That I was a
thing primarily. That I am not sure if I believed myself to be a
thing. Why I always said yes. Was it always for the food or
drinks? Or the chance to see something new? Maybe just a night
in the gaze.

I remember the dress and the boots and the haircut that night.
They were perfect together. You tell me I look like an "it girl,"
you cannot believe you get to take me out. I don't remember
where we go. Drinks. Wine maybe or cocktails. Maybe food. I
drink a little too much and you bring me back to your place in a
cab because you want to show it to me. I know now. I know. I
am enthusiastic. So big! So beautiful! You open the door to a
room you have just finished. A meditation room filled with

mandalas and bells. I take a step towards the door and you block me. *I'm sorry it is very expensive. You are not allowed in.*

Sitting on your couch waiting for a cab to take me home and we have not had sex and you are stroking from the top of my thigh down to my boot and saying, *you're lucky I'm such a good boy.* You're lucky I'm such a good boy.

This is a common thing for men to say to me. I am lucky, they tell me. I think about this. I am lucky. I, am lucky, that they, are such good boys. Lucky they debase me with their eyes? Lucky they rape me with their thoughts? Lucky they have made the decision, this one time, that they will not use their physical power to overcome me. That my entrance is sometimes as precious as the one to that kitschy overwrought room.

LIX

This one, I have no idea. You see me reading behind my desk at the gym and ask what I am studying in school. By now you are the fourth professor from my university who has taken an interest in me and these interactions have all ended the same, so I make assumptions from the start. I show you some of my writing. *You're not bad*, you say. You're a poet. A prominent member of the literary community. Your poetry is about trauma in your childhood. You tell me you are teaching a creative non-fiction class if I would like to audit it. I would, I say. You tell me you will give me a ride.

I sit in on a few of the classes. I remember the students but not much of the content. I remember you driving me there. We go on a trip to the Philadelphia Museum of Art, the Van Gogh exhibit. You buy me a ticket. My first time with *Rain* and you give me plenty of time to stand as close as I can to the paintings. Chronicle every brush stroke. Hours.

When I tell you I am leaving to live in Utah for some time you give me a gift. A tiger's blood stone. I quite like you and find you rather handsome but I do not touch you because I am not sure what this is and I think maybe it is what I was always looking for. Maybe this is mentorship.

I decide to apply for MFAs my final year of undergrad and I don't like the idea of bothering anybody. I reach out to you to see if you will write me a letter of recommendation. I send some work. You say. *This isn't like what I saw of yours before, I cannot recommend you.* And something else like, *this is not what I thought this was.* Or. *That was not what I believed the nature of our relationship to be.* Or. I don't know. I can't remember. But it stirs in me, disquiet. Self-doubt. The awareness that perhaps I am so unsure of my reality that anyone who sees me, my work, mocks me with praise because it is a sure way to be met with physical affection. It is an easy trick to play and guaranteed to work. Unless I am wrong. Projecting. Either truth seems just as likely. There are so many men that are like this and that I want to trust, like you A., want to believe, every time. You do not say explicitly you thought we were intimate. But, what would be worse? I have no idea.

LVI

Built from long nights lifting. Tan. But you say you like a different kind of woman. We chatter and drink at a bar for old men and after you bring me back to your apartment. We kiss and I try to fuck you, maybe suck your cock. *I'm not like that,* you insist. *I didn't know you were so young.* You let me sleep in your bed and you sleep on the couch with the dog. I leave in the morning before you wake and I admire your space. The window overlooking Rittenhouse. It is the same building I will have therapy sessions in years later. And I will smile walking past the doormen this time. Legitimate. When before sneaking out I could see their burning eyes. Careful of the rat.

XXI

We are beginning the quarantine and I worry. A friend let it slip
— *I thought you would like to know*. Cancer. A tumor? Is there a
name for cancers like this? *He doesn't know the name*, the friend
says. There must be a name. When you tell me about the
surgery you use the word leaking. You say, *I was still leaking*.
Without the g, or the g so soft as to walk away from the word
and it makes it all the more grotesque. Leakin-g. But the surgery
is not enough. You say you will know more in a week.

I did not think I would use the word you for everyone, but I have
to use it here. You are so wounded and fragile. You here is for
gentleness. You is not for questions. I have no more desire to
interrogate. Like you say. It was more than a decade ago and it is
all in the past. This is, partially true. But I know you are slow to
forgive, others, yourself. You hold low volume grudges in your
fist, years later opening your hand to see they have withered so
you hardly remember what they were. Your pretty white fingers
with the fine black hair along the knuckles. Wrinkled. Your feet
long too.

After a beach trip you are bedridden with sun poisoning,

covered in third degree burns. I tend to you. I feel your body like it is my body and I am ill with you.

I lie with my dog this morning, and it is like this. Without schedules there is no need to make concessions to the alarm so we spend a slow morning in the sun not knowing the time with her nose tucked beneath my chin. Massaging her neck, long pets on her back and ears. And doing this I feel my own stiff legs and jaw soften. My hip creases.

It is like this when I am with you. It is like our bodies are the same body.

Fucking everywhere. In my bathroom mornings before I drive you to school. In the car. In parks. In fields. Playgrounds. In your basement most often. You get little marks of my cum on your t-shirt because we never have time to undress. I wear small skirts. Like bunnies. Or, like teenagers. Eight, nine times an afternoon. I take your virginity in a cemetery. Sitting on your lap in our coats.

You say you are glad I reached out. You like to call now in the mornings before your radiation. The first time you ask me if you can call. My heart. It turns me to putty with grief that this softness was always there beneath the surface. The pain of you now forced to the point of overripe — vulnerable. How alone we both turned out to be.

Does a love so young matter? I have friends who idealize these affairs and say they never after have experienced anything so intense. If only I were so lucky. It matters, I think. I think we matter. Formative is the word here.

I fantasize about working. Going to law school and coming home to you. Stocking feet on plush carpet while you sit on the couch with a guitar and a child. I am imagining your mother's home I realize in this old fantasy. You've cooked dinner and smile and are sweet. I recognize now the fantasy is you A. You and your wife — when I thought I had lost this want so many years before. And I query here my intentions. If I cannot have this thing, if I am not good enough to have this thing, may I at least be its approximate?

Please, not asking the cost.

Yes the softness must always have been there but disguised as sadness which you were drenched in. Beneath the angry humor. The handsome smile. Deep unabating sadness, that maybe was always just this love — undernourished like the rest of you.

Even after you leave me we never stop fucking. How can we? How can we deprive our bodies of their own halves? I crawl naked into your bed on my twenty-first birthday after drinking three quarters of a bottle of Pear Absolut Vodka. Never mind my girlfriend. When I attend your shows I beckon, and you come. We fuck when we are both so thin I can wrap my hands around our waists. Seventeen in your dorm room. Twenty-four and you allow me to take your photo after. Twenty, Four Lokos and jumping on the bed. It doesn't feel like cheating. It just feels like our bodies being.

You did shatter me though. Christ you did.

The sound in your voice when I called. Weak. Vulnerable and low like a grieving animal. A little like a growl. When it had been almost seven years, and I would still sometimes hope.

The very mundane and normal history of us that makes it so tragic to hear from you now. After radiation you go to the beer distributor to work, even with the world upside down.

I am so afraid for you, already malnourished and isolated and now a breeze would take you out.

Maybe I am afraid to write this one because I don't want to write it again in a month. To add an addendum or, tempt something.

What matters? The book of CDs I still have of American Football and Bikini Kill and Weezer and the way I would irritate you by playing the same song over and over?

But if you love something you want it again and again ad infinitum.

It does not matter how we would take classes together just to sit beside one another. And you would, mischievously, put one earbud in my ear and leave one in yours and play a song. Usually The Beatles, "I Want to Hold Your Hand." How normal you made me, how solid the footing so I could be anything I chose, and what I chose, what I wanted, was to be was yours.

Does it matter that you left me? The manner? The reasons? Does it matter how much it hurt or that I never recovered my faith in all of this. I ask you just last night. Why did you leave me? The pain of it still lodged somewhere deep where I cannot shake it loose. My forehead against the cold tile of the bathroom, bloody nose, unable to stand just with the weeping after having seen you with her.

The times you weren't there don't matter. The porn you watched that I reviled doesn't matter. The essays I wrote for your English classes. My jealous possession. Listening to you fuck my ex-girlfriend in the room above me. Sick and alone and you brought me oranges. The simple songs you wrote that see me too clear. The way I needed so badly for you to be everything for me and the way you were still a boy and so could not.

The way you say, said always, stop letting them treat you like meat. *I don't like how you let them treat you.*

I hope this document can sit here and bring you wellness.

When I am hospitalized for appendicitis you are the one who stays by my bed. You sit by my bed for days and read *Ender's Game.* I love the look of the thick stacks of paper in your hands. The dark cover against the pale flesh. I love your hands. I love you. So different. Quieter. I wish I could have taken care of it all. I wish you would have let me.

XXV

A small cock. An accent I assumed was a speech impediment. A habit of burping into your fist after eating. You take me to your parent's home in the suburbs, they have a small above ground pool, and I change into my suit in front of you, offering. You turn away. Avert your eyes.

When I am in Tokyo I call you almost every night. When I return I think we will begin a real relationship. I think you will want to be with me, blubbering as I am. The intensity of the emotion at the time and I can barely think of enough to say about you to fill up three paragraphs.

You pick me up the night I fly back from Tokyo. You tell me in a Wendy's parking lot that you cannot be with me. I am simply, too much. I say hold me I'm sorry I think I have to cry? And you say, *I knew you would cry Sam.*

Who do I ever think I'm fooling.

LXXXIII

You, in contrast, have the biggest cock in this book. I say it with admiration and praise. I remember buying you coffee after our first night together and returning back to your apartment, holding the shaking cups, already cold from five minutes in the Montana air — you opening the door in the nude. How I managed not to drop them.

The only partner I've ever had who wanted more than me. I wish I'd had time to grow more adept with your body. I wish I wouldn't have been so afraid of you. The excitement that first time of seeing you in the window seat at the bar. That proud woman, waiting for me.

You point out the waitresses you've fucked later that year as we are catching up. Her. Her. Her. *I made her cum ten times in a night.* And you are so imitative of big rich Boomer men I cock my head back and laugh. You beg me to let you fuck you against your desk.

Holding my hand as we watch Hillary in the debates. A thrill, a squeeze.

LXIII

I'm sorry I can't remember your name. Truly abashed I cannot recall it. I want to blame the drugs.

In group one day, one of those groups where all ages and afflictions are tossed together in a large sharing circle and I am terrified of women and have no idea how to talk to them and so I just offer compliments roundly. Oh _____, so sweet with the handsome brother. Her eyebrows. I will return to the months here, some-where else. Don't look for any more in this volume.

But, caring for her as you did, you knew all my secrets. You helped me measure my food and write in my log. We drink non-alcoholic beer and watch movies and carve jack-o'-lanterns. Bike rides, but not too fast. You never push me for sex. We kiss. You finger me. Nothing more.

Years later you come to the wine bar I am working at. You are more handsome than I remembered. We go home and you finger me again but I won't allow sex. How much did I just love knowing that I could say no, so sure of the no working. As you touch me you look down with contempt, disgust.

XLIII

When I am drunk at the fancy graduation party in the suburbs
with the full roasted pig and the open bar and the couples
playing badminton — underage I have been snuck so much wine
that you put me in your car to collect later, someone trailing
behind you. You close the door and say to him, *tonight she's
mine.* Later that evening you try to call me back from the roof of
your parent's house where I might be naked, drinking the rain.
Running it along my skin. The next day writing poems about
my body near your pool in the sun. You say you want to
encourage my wildness, my strength and hedonism. But it
frightens you too. You like play. You like to tie women up, make
them cum with knives. You like to accommodate fantasies. You
love to play with so many partners. But, you hate it when things
get real. Our last time, just this year. Watching prestige television and drinking red wine and after you wallop me to the point
of welting with your belt. Playing. You ask me to cry out with
the pain but I don't want to. I just want to take it. I won't utter a
peep. And fucking a few days later. Dispassionate. You say I can
spend the night, our two bodies mismatched and the strength of
your body comes here with a hubris that makes the night outside

seem that much more frightening. That you don't know what is
out there.

We meet at a party. I am in attendance with the couple I am
dating. A charming photographer and a red headed bohemian. I
am their third and I like this very much, being taken out by the
two of them — being kissed by the two of them. They invited me
and I do not quite understand the rules of the party. This a
clever hipster crowd and everyone must attend in their under-
wear but I thought the goal was to look pretty, not cool. So while
most women are in boxer shorts and sports bras I'm in a strapless
black balconette and a pair of lace panties. Earrings. Eyeliner.
You shadow me. Enormous. And you strike me as dangerous.
Smoking cigarettes and kissing, nearly catching a strand of long
red hair on fire. You are orbiting. When the three of us move to
go you physically separate me from the pair, block my way
down the hall. *I'd be pursuing the hell out of you right now.* I am
unimpressed.

But, later.

Our relationship over the past decade is mostly correspondence.
We are lonely. We are sad. One of us is contemplating or
attempting suicide. Then we are angry. I never remember what
we are angry about. One of us cuts off communication. Incredibly petty disagreements that lead to years without contact.
After one such fight — a fight over your denim which is of such
high quality you keep it in the freezer overnight and which I
mock mercilessly — you walk right past me, without a glance. As
if I do not even exist. As if I only exist when you allow me to.

You pressed so hard and pulled so quick. Driving on highways
after too much whiskey screaming Flogging Molly lyrics. Like
you are invincible. Like you can make me invincible too if I can
only find a little faith.

XCII

You're very pretty, I hate to offend. But it was always your partner I wanted to fuck.

LXXXVI

A long brunch near the West Loop. A diner with big windows. Red gingham tablecloths. A couple down the bar eating chicken and waffles. You live at the furthest South end of Chicago and I the furthest North, it will be our undoing. But for now, so pretty with such small hands. You have only been with men. Your husband and you have been open for some time though and you are excited to try. I am relieved, you will not notice my inexperience. With your small hands you make shapes. You teach me ASL. You let me touch one of the expressive verbal fingers. We walk along the river and kiss in the center of a bridge and on our next date we hold hands openly walking down the street. I put my arm around you. I order us both a glass of Beaujolais.

XXXVIII

When I am abandoned in Nagano — the man who does the abandoning a large chapter I have cut to accommodate my bruises and pettiness — I buy a ticket to take an earlier train home alone. You see me and say, *why don't you sit in business class with me?* Do you buy me my ticket? Your English is not bad but still we rely often on a small translator you have in your bag. A proper businessman in a suit and everything. You ask if when we get back to Tokyo I would like to go out to dinner? I agree. I go home shower, groom, meet you at a fancy sushi restaurant in Shinjuku where we eat pricey sashimi over ice and drink sake and I am glad not too much. When we go out onto the streets you kiss me but not a gentle kiss, a forceful demanding kiss, and grip my body and *there is a love motel nearby*, something about strong women. I do not comply, I run again. When do I unlearn the word no. Regain it. Only safe when I'm on the train.

A photo of me another night. A yellow cardigan and wine stained lips, looking down, pressed between bodies so I can barely touch the floor on the looping Yamanote. Another here.

In a black dress vomiting in front of the bright Astro Boy mural in my neighborhood. A briefcase is put down. Gentle murmuring from inside a stiff white shirt and a hand runs from my shoulder to the middle of my back, paternal, stroking and calming — maybe, *you'll wake up tomorrow.*

A.

I have no pride. How to want this living.

I beg you, please. Please.

You chose her. You choose her every day.

XLI

Sometimes I would call you by your given name, and you liked
it. The last thing I ask you, am I a human being?

You never respond.

We are relief to have found one another. You say I am broken
inside the way you are broken outside and I touch your scars
along your face and chest and kiss your ears. You are a bit of a
legend. The year before we meet you are doing drugs in a
majestic old hotel abandoned for most of my youth, and you
take a wrong step. You fall, is it fifteen stories? No, I've just
found an article, it is five down an elevator shaft. You survive,
but barely, with seams up your legs, a stiff walk, hearing aids.
Dizzy visions and visitors from morphine that haunt you. You
trace them for the rest of use to see in black and white drawings.
When we meet you have not yet begun to truly mend.

You paint me. "After Sex Avocado." Topless in pink panties
eating half of the green fruit with a spoon. My hair in the
painting long over my face. My thighs thin. I believe I offered

you some. And we are happy to be together in this too. The sex occurs at a different frequency for us. We both see it it just as sex and a physical action, and it is a relief not to have to wear the mask of titillation or emotion. Just something we are good at, or used to. We fuck and it is enthusiastic but whenever we feel like taking a break, we do. I will get a snack downstairs and bring it up to eat or I will write a poem or we will talk. You walk down Broad St. late at night with boxed wine or whiskey to protect me from the nightmares. You cook for me. You say you will have me over anytime, a person with so much gratitude, so much delight for your cooking? *I'll make you anything.*

You are, someone I regret I did not slow down enough to grow with.

Just seeing you on the street one day after we are long over, begging you to come with me. We fuck too many times when we are over and each of them it is me, desperate to feel the connection to something as broken as I am again. But you are becoming bigger, more full. You are finally healing while I am splintering deeper and wider. Halfway through this time I begin weeping while you are still inside of me. You remind me of this later. *I'd never seen anyone cry that way, so animal.* You say. *I thought to myself — this is what it is to be a human.*

Your work. Abstract and messy. Hot. Advanced. You tell me when you use green that it is me. I am glad that you know me, that despite all the time that has passed you have not forgotten my essence. There is of course, no green anymore. Red. Red. Red. Red. White, a little yellow. Black. And so much red. Eating the canvas the red. I imagine your wife must be red. You tell me you can no longer continue talking to me, to protect her. I say I understand, but I am crying. I ask. Was any of it real? You confirm, *it was real, but.* Apparently your wife and I have shared another lover. She is wounded, jealous. You are a good man protecting her and it hurts me to see you grown so far.

So many end this way with good men protecting women who are good and worthy of protection. Protecting them from, my existence? Even the times when I feel I have done nothing wrong.

Must I simply stop being? Or, must I behave more quietly to help you all in your chivalrous mission. Should I avert my eyes? Cover my ankles? Must I always cry alone. Must I always say goodbye to those I love for their benefit. Women who are feminists who don't want me anywhere near them. Sometimes it is not even just me. Women who say they love women who will not let their man speak to anyone with tits who is not them. Leftist women who lay down laws like Pence's mother.

But, this also in a way means you are the type of man you wanted to become. Every time we would pass someone looking for a dollar or a smoke you had something to give. You did it with friendly banter no matter how poor you were. This man was always there.

I wonder if you are disappointed that I have not kept up with your steady progress. Maybe you think I want to stay that broken little thing that was capable of being beautiful to someone like you — porcelain in your scarred fingers. If you only see beauty in the cracks. Again, if I emerge from this mire. Seamless.

The last thing I ask you.

But, look there. If you know the name of the painting and if you go back to when the artist was younger you will see. I was there. I existed. There are pieces of green. _____, who I revisit often. I wonder where I am and what you are thinking of. If you are thinking of my fingers on your chest. Drinking whiskey and watching *Barfly*, the woman at the bar with Bukowski, wondering to one another why we are watching ourselves. Disillusioned with jagged open sores, and young. A perfect broken pair. But, look. _____. There too I can be seen behind the clouds. If I am disappeared now. Look. Look, there I was though.

LXXVIII

All you wanted was for me to pee on you. Cooking dinner. And
I so sheepish, just stuff yourself inside of me, like that is less
grotesque. A black pen. Soup. A story from your ward at the
Children's Hospital but you just want to cook all day. And you
have Leukemia, and that is the last I hear.

VIII

Teenagers. Standing in a field after your suicide attempt you run your hands over the front of me and down inside my pants and just finger me, one finger, standing like that. You say it is the most sensual thing.

XXVII

Freshman year I ride a train to visit an old friend, an old beau also otherwise absent from this text, who lets me cry and gets me drunk and buys me a famous bowl from a combined Taco Bell and KFC. Heady with the calories. It is a small town and the kind of party I have not been to since high-school. Drop outs and teen parents and indoor smokers in a one floor house at the end of a cul-de-sac.

Towards the end of the night I am happy. Smiling with the pleasure of human company and weed. My disposable camera is making the rounds. I don't remember meeting you or talking to you, but I remember seeing you, wanting you, being warned about you. But I wanted you horribly. A trucker, if I remember correctly. If I think about you now, you must have been in your late twenties, more likely your thirties. I am warned you like them young, but I look younger than I am and I never tell you my true age of nineteen so you can assume what you want. You have shoulder length blonde hair and a bit of a beard — prominent abs with criss-cross guns tattooed over them just above the groin.

I remember that tattoo distinctly and nothing of the cock below, neither its appearance nor the quality of the intercourse. I was wildly enamored though with the tattoo.

The full house, when I state my desire, gifts us a bedroom.

You do not like that I am experienced. I don't care.

Mid-coitus the door is opened, a photo is snapped. I develop it at a CVS. You can see my splayed left leg and your ass. Nothing else.

We sleep on the couch together and in the morning, even hearing voices in the kitchen, I crawl down under the blanket we share to suck you off. Empowered. I don't know your name and I never hear from you or see you again.

Mostly the guns, this one is for the guns — how even now I am again obsessed with the look of them on the thick lower abdominals. "Cum gutters." And it is not an obsession of want, but of envy.

IV

A.

I am in proximity. I am in close proximity.

I am in proximity as the wife grows round with new love. I am
in proximity for the ultrasounds. I am in proximity for the birth,
your flushed cheeks at the coffee shop. A boy. A name. A sun
sign.

I am in proximity as the boy grows. I am in proximity as your
family grows. I meet the boy. I love the boy. I am often in proximity to the boy in your home. He is like you and I understand
why people want this, to create more of the people they love. I
do not approve but when I hold him for the first time I think, I
truly understand her desire. My desire an approximate to hers.
You say you would like me to be closer, inside the family instead
of existing only as an itinerant non-resident. But, the barrier
never breaks and still I am circling like a predator — searching
for a fissure I might slide through. You tell me later how you do
not trust me.

I am still in proximity. I am in proximity to your home full of
music and intellectual banter and food. I am in proximity to the

world of people you love who must stand outside your home even now just to be closer to your grace. I am in proximity as I sit alone and write this. Or paint. Or teach my students blue essays about conquering grief, telling them through Ross Gay to wander into a wilderness of sorrows and find joy. But they must know it is flat. *It is too sad*, they say. *Where is the joy?* I say again, through the sorrows, as if I can be convinced myself.

I am in proximity to joy. I am not permitted to touch it.

I am in proximity as you fix your marriage. I am in proximity as you sit up at night and tell her you love her, as you listen to her pain. I am in proximity as you hold her hand and promise you will never hurt her like this again. Crying. I am in proximity as you promise her you are staying. *I chose you. I love you.*

You choose her. You love her.

I love the life we have built.

I am here.

I am in proximity as you touch each other, grateful to be close. A true love. I am in proximity.

I am in proximity.

LXXXV

You tell me he was afraid before he went. A man of faith. And I shiver and cry and hold your head against my stomach.

Will some of these years not just pull into the earth like water into soil?

If I have gained a quality from each of these interactions. Perhaps I gain from _____, skepticism, aesthetic cruelty. Perhaps I gain from you, A., clarity and a confirmed resignation. And here? You put me in touch with my pathetics. My pleading and my desperate squirming wants. Waving as we exchange goods. You smile like we have not both threatened to take this to court. Like I am not afraid of you. Or, like we are not afraid of each other.

We spend our last Christmas together in your apartment. I make mulled wine. Skyping with your family while your father is in hospice care. You fly out the next day and he passes almost as soon as you land.

Your grief. Had we not deteriorated so far. I tried to hold your pain. I did not do enough. Need I remind you reader, I am not good? I am not looking to be forgiven?

I sit with a friend a few days later. We get breakfast Guinness and stew. Another friend of mine dies on the same morning as your father, they die within a few hours of one another. And, I just want to feel warm. The year since the election has aged me so that even the features of my face are harsher. I develop alopecia and cut my hair short again, the hairdresser saying they will do their best to cover up the large chunks of missing hair on the back of my head. So much loss, of life, of hope, of identity. I just want to feel warm.

You list me in the obituary you write for your father as your life partner and our dog as our child. I am very gentle but I tell you, you cannot do this. You know that is not what we are. You know we are over. And you say, yes I know. But in a way that makes me certain you do not. Our realities are so far removed.

The first time I can't even go through with the task, filling out the forms with the help of an aid and then saying. Maybe I'll come back. Leaving. You finding me again.

When I return to the courtroom the same aid as before sees me, ushers me in eagerly, glad I've returned. Sitting in the court's waiting room I re-read *Conflict is Not Abuse*. There are televisions but none of them are on. The furniture is hard. Most of the women are crying. And it is all women. Some with children. Some with mothers or friends. The ones with mothers in particular I rest on, enviously. I am masculine and hard and alone, not crying. Too afraid to be weak in this public place.

The judge wears a polka dot tie.

The first order merely temporary. Now you have the right to contest. And, returning.

The pews remind me of a religious ceremony of some kind. And the look of you. You aren't wearing socks. Your ankles vulnerable. In the same shoes I chose for you years ago. The same style, a different pair. Later, finding me. Is the fear rational, I can ask myself now. But then I could not look back over my shoulder, running around Wrigley Park in heels, drenched in sweat in November.

There is only one other party who contests. A couple. There are three judges today and one of them asks the woman, *are you sure you feel safe with him?* And the woman says, *I am carrying his child, what choice do I have?* And so the order of protection is lifted without any further questioning.

And one day. When you are tired and just enough on the edge? I read the statistics. I know where stalking usually ends. Just waiting every day for it. Wondering when and if. And also if I am insane.

A memory. Early.

A vacation in Bozeman. A night in a bed and breakfast and a day in the town. Real restaurants and bookstores. Things I miss from cities. And also the mountains sprawling around us. Nestled so safe inside them. Walking home from our drinks and I jump up wrapping my legs around your waist. Kissing you while you carry me down the road.

LI

When you finally see my body you laugh. *I was worried you would be too thin. But, no. You have a warrior's body.*

My cheeks red with offense. But you are not wrong.

Fucking on the roof only one limb on any surface at any given time. A hand. A foot. A knee. Like we are acrobats.

You are gloriously beautiful with your blonde hair — with your perfect teeth and clear blue eyes. But there is something about the softness of the skin of men who look like this. With their biceps and pectorals and their chiseled jaws. The flesh of them always smells sour to me. Always is too soft and hairless to be paired with their member.

Everyone finds you beautiful, tells me I should be struck by you. I see that you are chiseled, alluring, yes. Charismatic, yes. But it does not move me the way it seems to move others. And perhaps this intrigues you. My roommate after meeting you the once will ask, *what happened to that ___,* as she is unimpressed with the string of men I lead in and out after you, all of a more middling appearance. My grandmother when she meets you, of all things, *flirting* with you. *You remind me of my father in his Naval uniform.* Still inquiring after you all these years later. My sister's deep crush on you in high-school. When I say your name and she looks up from her work. *You know him?*

And sitting with you and my extended family is when I realize I can no longer try to be a part of them. When I realize the pain of them is not worth the blood ties. They see you in a way they cannot see me. My doting grandmother and my uncle asking about your travels. Asking about your films. Never once looking at me. And the way they push me on you, hoping for us to multiply and replenish. What intolerable children we would make. Your entitlement and blind optimism paired with my brooding and pain and all dripping with a dazzling Aryan prettiness. I can think of nothing more revolting than something half yours growing inside me. And I quite like you.

I want my grandmother to love me like she loves you. Like I am a man. Like I am a person with a mind and I feel the ages of old want and the way I am dismissed. The way they all take so easy to you as though the sight of us together makes me palatable. They do not know what to do with me when I am alone, where to seat me, or what to say to me. Pushing into my arms babies babies babies. And then one year in my mid-twenties, I am too strange for the babies. Without gender in my spinsterhood. Walking from the kitchen to the basement. *No, no, this is only for the boys. The girls are upstairs with the children.* And looking at you, less brilliant than me, at least then, less traveled and versed. But similar enough to what I might be like as a man. And they take to you so well just upon this first meeting. And I am invisible after years away, existing only in your shadow.

After this trip I never go back to Utah.

We take the train out together from Philly and you promise an

Amish man who has seats behind us that you will not kiss me, that you are good and chaste. But after whiskey from a coffee cup I show you a chapter of my novel and you say this is not art. *This is a grotesquerie.* And I say it is life. And you are shocked I could even think of such filth. Smut. You ask me how I can even think of *such* filth. You kiss me beneath a blanket.

You say I inspire you to travel, that I am the moment when you decide — *that's someone who is actually doing it.* And you are so disappointed that while I run and run I am bleak in my soul when you had been anticipating a kindred spirit, someone glittering with a lust for life. And, strangely, though you like existing so much, you are averse to physical lust. Or, my lust. I am as dark as you are light and you cannot fathom it.

One night in college I open the door and let out the band that has stayed over, the bassist who kept me warm the night before smiling and waving goodbye. You are on my front stoop, I believe you have slept there, with your, god, was it a pan flute? No, worse. A melodica. Your traveler's clothes. It is winter. You have a gift for me though, an offering. Two bus tickets to the beach and, yes, we know. Whiskey again. Gin. You write a song about me called "Sin and Tonic." Walking along the shore and into the waves in the winter. I'm wearing men's pants and a blazer and we might kiss, I'm not sure, but I know we talk. The water this night is so beautiful with Atlantic City's lights reflected. I love Atlantic City, the trash of it paired with the natural wonder. As I said, I love the ocean. I love walking into the ocean and deciding, today, because you are so lovely, I will not walk all the way.

In a casino we put all our money on one number and make friends with an older couple who take us up to their room and you smoke something with them, there might be cocaine, and they try to proposition us. In the corner the man asks me to take off my clothes while you laugh. After you ask, *who does stuff like*

this? I do, I say. And on the bus back late at night we watch the
film that inspired you to make films and we drink out of a bottle
in a brown bag and you sleep over and smell like the ocean and
take off your shirt but we do nothing more than lie like this. And
_____ who is in the room and watches us sleep tells me, *oh Sam,
he is so lovely.* And, I suppose. I am grateful for the sand in the
bed. I do not want to clean it out.

You have been abroad for years making your film, all over the
world, and so when I first see you this past January, crouched
outside the art museum in that same leather jacket, I think I am
hallucinating. And after, he will not remember me. I am too
changed. But you come closer and closer at the Women's
March, always behind your camera. It is snowing and the flur-
ries are around your cheeks and the halo of your hair and I say
your name. Putting the camera down. Smiling. You rush at me
and we collide like a panel from a comic book — so violent and
quick the embrace that a cloud of dust might have flown up
between us. And I have missed you. We stand to the side of the
march, fumbling with small talk. I tell you I am teaching. I
promise you not to fuck up bright young filmmakers. You offer
me mimosa in a water bottle. I love this, that you are still the
same. You tell me you want to just sit and talk, trade stories.
You're flying back to Berlin in two days. But you are so far
beyond me now. Your life has grown where mine has dwindled.
I don't want you to see the way my world has become nothing
but a series of quiet pains that you would not be able to comprehend. Strangers to each other. You let me take a photo of you in
front of the museum steps. It is a good photo. You are more
rugged in your beauty now and I like it this way.

I walk up the steps a few minutes later, returning to the
galleries. I don't turn around but I hope you see me. I hope you
watch me.

LXV

Almost every woman I meet traveling, when we sit and talk. A
formative sexual assault. So maybe we are out and alone
because we presume to know the worst when perhaps we
cannot truly fathom. Bright green rice fields. Cigarettes — the
smoke blending with your white blonde hair.

LXXXIX

The day is so long thinking only of Kavanaugh Kavanaugh Kavanaugh. At noon I call a friend for lunch, which becomes a Guinness and Jameson. Another Jameson. Another. Was I expecting them to play the hearings on the television in the Irish pub? The conversation is rambling, but it returns and returns to sexual violence.

I feel camaraderie with my friend, with our server who pours us a round on the house. *On a day like today.* My friend shares a story of assault. I share one. I share the story of you and the bar and the maybe assault, asking, what is this? How am I so old and I still do not always know.

Their partner drives me home. They are not a drinker and I can feel them judging, as though I am a sullying influence. I will fuck them later too so maybe I am.

That night I sit in a chair and watch all of the hearing. I listen to the coverage unable to sleep. Kavanaugh is worse than the election somehow. Kavanaugh puts me in my place then and every day since. Kavanaugh reminds me my pain is laughable while his is, yours, is real. Indelible in the hippocampus. And this story relates to you too A. Your "real" life, so much bigger and therefore so much more meaningful than mine. Like mine is imagined by you or some other man. My lack of attachments. My gender. My hysteria.

You are studying at the same school as me. Every semester or so we get a drink. Talk. It is platonic. You are a painter. We meet on this evening and sit in the owner's booth accidentally but he tells me I am foxy so we can stay. You tell me you cheat on your girlfriend. I tell you I had an affair with our boss. *That dinosaur?* You say I always was attracted to you. I say I want to smash. We take a cab to my place.

I am too drunk. Whiskey dick and I remember taking off my clothes but when you ask me, jokingly, *are we cuddling?* I do not know how long we have been on the bed. For the first time in years, the spins. This is the part. When you flip me over and start to choke me while inside me from above and I am pulling at your hands but then I am also frozen. It is the full weight of you choking me, pressing down on the front of my neck. I am in pain and can't breathe and I am sure this is how I am going to die and all I can think to do is be as still and amenable as possible. I tell myself, be as calm, as attractive as possible, as my vision blurs.

I don't know when choking was added to the short list of necessary acts in porn but it is now mainstream in a way it was not when I was young. But this time too, you choked to maim.

I cry the next morning on the phone, unsure, blaming myself. *Did I do something bad?*

Is it a punishment? If the heft of our bodies were reversed?

If two people engage in crimes — I am coercive. I know you have a partner and I want you, just to alleviate the hollow ache for even an hour. And, you are violent. You have a want too. Who decides which power is more power? Is it a nod to the patriarchy to find the masculine strength of forearms and hands more damaging than a wanton disregard for morality? A pathetic craving for flesh? Who decides which of us consented and to what extent? Is there another way to frame this? Another way to talk about it? I am only allowed to question this frame because it is mine, knowing that I am crossing a line perhaps. Perhaps this level of gradation does no one any favors?

I tell you this was bad. You apologize. You call me from Chicago to say you love me. Too high. But still you say I am the love of your life.

You say, after apologizing again — but. *I wanted so much.*

LXXV

When I return from Turkey — early, sick with depression, heart-break, and pneumonia — I take a yoga class with my sister. I will not attend her church services but I will mollify her in this way. The instructor approaches me after. *I have a son and he needs someone,* "different."

You have a car.

We go to a bar and you drink Diet Coke and I drink beer and when I mock you a bit too harshly you take a brash sip of my IPA and try not to make a face. You look like good Mormon stock. Blonde hair blue eyes a stiff uprightness that shows you served your mission. What are you trying to prove to yourself, to me?

XLIX

A hike in winter with sack lunches along a lake and you hold a
map in the snow, tall green trees every way in a circle. I follow
wherever you lead. Or, after a night out and you guide me all
the way back to my home, my bicycle behind yours. Telling me
when to stop. When to go. Which way to turn. Occasionally
using your own wide hand on my handlebars to steer for me
when I am confused.

The ways in which you are so smart. And the ways in which
you are not. You bring me a chocolate chip muffin when you
drive me to inpatient. As though. Such a sweet foolish gesture.
*What if the food isn't very good? Won't you be hungry if they
don't feed you until this evening?* A fluttering in my heart now.
You sit with me during the initial intake. I send you home before
I get into my hospital gown for the blood work. *Sometimes*, the
center tells me, *it is nice to have a friend with you.* I say. I can do
this alone. Young idiot does not know how tired she will become
of that word. In their life. In this godforsaken manuscript. You
always come back though. You visit more than anyone else and
we sit in the grass near the gazebo in my favorite red skirt and

you tell me about your life outside. When I tell you, thank you, years later. *I couldn't leave you all alone in that place.*

Visiting you in DC and meeting your new partner. She is beautiful. Refined. Poised. So small and feminine. The way you look at her. Just this past Thanksgiving you visit and I bring you to my favorite bar. Walking there she is in mittens. Her tiny mittened hand in yours. God, my heart. How can I feel, seven, at least seven different things, looking at her little hand in yours.

The first time I visit you in DC you set aside a whole room for me to spend the night. You never give me the accommodations I would settle for but instead the ones you think I deserve. Any person would deserve. Always assuring me I am just as good as any other person.

A date, maybe our only real date, at a five-star restaurant and there is something wrong with the order and you send it back and I am aghast. Blushing. Apologizing. But, you say you want me to get what I want. You say that I deserve to get what I want.

On the first bed that first visit made just for me and one night of my sleep, I look at you. Soft. Wishing I could keep it in. I'm still in love with you. And you look down with pity. *Oh. Oh.* Nothing more. And, up all night. Alone in the pristine bedding thinking of the two of you together in the room next to me. Happy she is good, someone I genuinely like. And also. Ugly with regret.

I am like a stray cat when we meet. Unkempt and poorly fed. Sometimes in Center City, between jobs, or before or after a date, knocking on your door. And if you are there you let me up. And sometimes we are friendly and watch cartoons or you show me a new project you are working on. You are a designer. I am something akin to a little brother, reading to you about Jennifer's body from your metal spiral staircase. Sometimes you are in the middle of cocktails or dinner and I partake. And sometimes it is sex. You never know which it will be and neither do I until the mood strikes me. I don't know how this began. I would not call ahead but simply arrive on your doorstep at odd hours.

I should say here how handsome you are. Perhaps the most handsome man I've ever been with. Not perhaps. Without question. Exquisite. The kind of stud used for breeding.

I am surprised the sex gets better the more you know someone. You tell me this and it is true. And. Stopping you. No, no, it feels too good. And you insist, *that's the point*. And I don't know yet that sex can be climbing up to the peak of pleasure and dropping off the other side.

In my late twenties when I first start cumming, and only by myself, hitting that crest of goodness feels itself like a pain. Like an acute jolt of agony. So for a long time after I've discovered how, I don't want to do it. Made so uncomfortable by delight. Confounded by the pressure and hurt of satisfaction. And it still seems like such a separate thing. Lately I've begun cumming to office furniture, the morning news, certain conversations in the early 2019 primaries, a single breast still covered by a shirt. Cumming to sex is much more difficult. Maybe sometimes. When I am in the mood to watch a woman's ass stuffed, or watch her humiliated. When I am angry or sad. But when I just want to cum it is easier to look at an old red phone. A lecture from the London School of Economics. Think of your cheek A., or ear, or some other part of your face. Sex and this kind of intimacy seem inherently incompatible to me. I tell you I am discovering this and you mock me. *Well, maybe I'll start reading to you from the New York Times.* Don't tease me. Melancholy.

We fuck like this for years but it is not until I am well into recovery, once I've navigated my cocktail of meds, once the crying fits have ebbed and I am writing papers and attending classes like I am sane — the weight heavy on me. Once I've done these things, standing on my kitchen counter feeling giddy with the joy of being free of my worst parts, talking to you on the phone.

_____, _____, _____! I love you!

I know. And. I love you too.

And after. A quiet few months. The aforementioned dinner where after we kiss near the park and I fall asleep on your chest on the couch. A weed brownie that makes us become one person. A night in your uncle's apartment which overlooks the parkway — a green dress. You stand behind me in a mirror and I realize suddenly I am much smaller than you. And as I said, you are so handsome.

A night of food poisoning where I vomit in your bathroom and the next morning you don't ask me to leave. The studio impossibly small so you can hear everything. I'm so sorry, so humiliated. You settle me on your couch with a thick blanket and make me oatmeal with berries. *Oh, Peeps. It sounded awful.* I could write a book just of sweet memories. It is not an exaggeration. I could write a book about the humanity you offer me.

So many of these have lapsed into nostalgia. Barely containing any narrative form. I wonder, do they seem coherent? Do you see the value to them? Do they resemble something in your own life and so can forgive me this stringing together of happy bits? Thank you for bearing with me. I love this one.

We are drinking in Center City and it has started to rain — suddenly everyone rushing under alcoves and there is a big brass band of maybe five or six people playing and you look at me and shout, gripping me, *Never forget the band!* Giddy with life. The way you see the world. I reach to you still for clarity. For understanding. Why am I so dense, the pain so enormous. *Maybe it is not bad you feel so much. Maybe it is a gift.* Burning up from the insides with hurt. Walking along the edge of the bridge with hurt. And later. *He's married. He's never going to want you back, or want you as much as he wants her. We can talk about it all you want, but. It is never going to change.*

A call earlier this month after too much wine. Is there something about her, your girlfriend? Am I a different species, less? Where in the system do *I* lie, or must it be a personal failing? Must it be my fault? And you never get angry but you never indulge. And I only ask every other year or so. Maybe every two and a half years. I want you to be happy. But I want to understand. How to understand that, like you A., he will never want me back, will never want me as much as he wants her. I can ask why all I want. But, it is never going to change.

XCIII

You are so beautiful, I can never see you again. You are so beautiful and you smile so pretty and dangerous when you let me pull your hair behind your ear at the bar and you tell me, *I hate art I love paint I love line* — it makes me so goddamned wet. You tell the bartender this is an excellent first date and let me choose your beer for you and after when you buy the man a full dinner you are so worried you did not ask what kind of soda he wanted. I am a cynic. I'm sure an XL Coke will be fine. But you are so worried you want him to get exactly what he wants. You hold my hand for just a little bit and I kiss you so hard like I want to eat you when you go down to the train.

I call you, A., when she is submerged, to tell you I might be happy with someone who isn't you and you are upset, jealous. But while I am still dizzy with confusion you hang up and return to your wife's dinner party.

You, A., are not kind to people who are houseless. Sharp and dismissive. Sometimes not even looking at them. It is one of the only things about you I don't love. Actively hate. I always thought it was your wife's influence, but perhaps it was a red

flag for how you perceive certain humans. Those whose circum-
stances have left their world's a bit emptier than yours. Maybe it
should have been clear to me that I too would end as waste
to you.

I do not see you again. My priorities are clear to me. How do I
explain I am in love with someone. I am not sure you will share
me. You struck me as possessive. Our affair struck me as
consuming. And I don't want to lose you A., the boy. Not again.
Not so soon. Not even for her.

A.

I tell them. This is the morning I haven't bought the gun for.
They tell me, *it is hard for you, but, if you say it again I'm going
to have to call the cops.*

Standing in the shower. Showering two, three times a day.
Wishing I knew how to drown. Incompetent even in this want.
A painting. Hands over a body in a shower. Baby blue hands.
Another painting. A woman reclining, hovering, a crouch and
also a rest. Her right breast exposed to the viewer and the paint
is thin near the center of the meat so it is like a light comes from
inside her. A white figure, bigger, hunching, leaning over, lips
extended to kiss the highest arch of the front her neck — which
you could slice with a wire. A line of thick black, of empty
space, between the man's lips and the woman's chin. As though
the black touches each of them. As though the space is dense
and part of their touching their closeness their want. But, thin
enough to taste the space on either side where they are apart.
Death. On the far left. Laughing. Death's hand supporting the
slenderest bit of the woman's back.

And life too, on the right. Headless.

Music to cover the relentless weeping the talking in the mirror for the neighbors. You are here. You are right here. To the mirror. You are here. Touching the body seeing the person who is you touch the body. You are right here. Cambodian rock from the '60s. No don't think about the torture. The body. The nipples. The lesions. The photos. The bodies. All dead. The stack of the musician's bodies. The empty spaces in the sounds. The circles of pavement the market. The circles of pavement the market. Aerial view then slipping amongst the pillars running and laughing and you remember the smell of the fish and the heat. Trying to say, in the now, "I am here," to the streets as you begin to sob by the trash cans. Streets emptied from the virus which remind you of the photos again and then suddenly a man in a mask with a son. I am here. I am here. I am here.

No matter the boy's age no matter the look of the father. Sweating. Gulping for air that is not wet with you A. Orange robes and hot. And the circles of pavement and the market.

Our last night. When you stand with me in the shower I am so cold and you touch me and you tell me, *but no sex I just want to touch* and you say, *why can't we just lie together?* But I don't want to get out of the water drinking beneath the hot stream and standing like that I feel the loss of you. The loss at the end of the summer. The sudden black space where before there was.

The thick black line between our faces on the street. The whole world is hot with my want to cross the line to touch.

Can I again use the word love? This is too painful to be love. The way you left me is not love. What you have with them is love. Whatever we had was something else. Maybe just void. What exists before void. When now there is only void. What is before.

And we fight. You tell me, *you are impulsive. You lack boundaries and patience. Do you like that she is threatened by you?* I beg you not to look below my shoulders.

You ask why I want to punish you. I tell you it is not meant to be torture, but that there are consequences to your leaving.

You tell me to look at how good you have been. You tell me, *you have to trust me.*

You, touching my breast, and I cannot feel the hand like my skin has turned to callus. So eager to be in the scalding water with me you leave the key in the door. Forgetting.

But we are already dead.

And when I consent and lie with you and touch my hand to your cheek as you cry, as I cry, and you say. *Will it help with the pain if I have sex with you?* And I say yes when I mean no. But I have been begging for you the whole night, and so you must think you are doing a service. And you fuck my body like it used to be fucked by you. And I am in my body, I suppose I must be. And this too feels like mourning. And I ride you and hold your hands above your head. And you tell me it feels so different. You tell me it does not work for you the way it used to, and I don't know how to tell you it is because I am not there, that I don't know how to find a way back into my body after your betrayal. When you are finished you are hungry, not for me but for food. Your body longs for sustenance elsewhere as I have not given it enough.

You leave me like this, lying naked in the bed, and you never return.

And the bed to my left. And the same walls. And the same shower. And I am here every day looking at the gravesite. And I am here every day sleeping in the grave. Too much sun in the windows. Outside endless channels of empty pavement. Grids. But, wavering.

And you leave.

A letter I keep on yellow paper. You sit with me before returning to your child. Why can't I give you to him willingly when it means you are good? When it is good. I refuse the martyrdom offered me to instead remain a parasite.

The letter is written in all caps on yellow paper. Your wife must know this is how you write, must be so intimate with this writing. A shopping list. A love letter. An apology. A note so you don't forget. A photo of her sitting on a hotel bed. Young. A shiny sleeveless dress. Brightness between you, the way she looks at the camera. The look mortar.

In the letter you say you can do nothing to help me deal with the pain. But you think of me. You say better, when you mean worse.

You leave. And before you leave I am stroking the tears from your cheek.

The skin along your jaw, loose. The tears. And. Your cheek in my hand. Your cheek in my hand. And. You leave.

My own hand to my own cheek. To the mirror. You are here. You are here.

Your neck beneath the cheek. I have spent too little time thinking of the neck that supports the grace.

LXXXIV

In Montana and you hold me close, pecs and abdominals, once just our nipples touching. The tips of our noses. Holding my hand under a table while I meet your colleagues.

After, sitting in your car. *Can I play you something I wrote?* An EP, song after song about your obsessive love for another woman driving in circles, a small sob. Then, dropping me off. Not a word about it after.

LXXXI

On our second date, before fucking. Crying on my shoulder.

Walking past the open window and the dog catching her scent and the moans you knew so well. More tears.

Why did she leave me?

XCI

You say I am too young. Head against your chest, discussing cannibalism. My desire to be consumed. Looking down as you eat my lips, pulling at them between your teeth like gristle off of bone — holding easily the weight of my entire torso as I convulse with deliciousness, uncontrollable. The taste of myself pooled in your mouth.

Moving your leg in your hip socket after sex. Your joints. The long deep scar that runs across your chest. A near fatal accident and long curly hairs I've been finding throughout the quarantine. We exchange a few sentences, a new piece of our lives, a reference to a film only important to one of our generations, then we fuck again. Vigorously. Well and animal you fill me exactly, the perfect shape. Before the sun sets you usually go home. Still, every time you chatter about your wife who you say you are leaving. Have left. I say I worry.

You bring me gifts. An ice cube tray. Apples. Rye whiskey. Camembert. A photo of your hard cock which you have printed onto a sheet of white paper. I have an affinity for the member. The gesture not graphic but instead sweet.

The first night it is maybe 2am and I have completed a syllabus for the class I am teaching and I am proud of it and I want to reward myself. I have found you online. I want you. I tell you to drive across the city, fuck me now. You do. When I see you standing outside my door I am pleased. Tall and thick and a sweetness to your face. We both smile.

Pushing me against the counters, malleable beneath your working hands, almost thoughtlessly forceful but never unkind. Again, again. You say, *god you're actually beautiful. How did I get so lucky?* That is a pleasure in and of itself. The first time you try to hit me at my request and are too inept at unkindness and also too strong.

This last time, looking at the wall. You like to mock my paintings. I say I know I'm not very good. You were a painter before you were a carpenter. You show me some of your work. It is all quite lovely. Quite heterosexual. *Is this man holding the baby the one you're still crying over?* Groaning and turning my face into the pillow.

LXXVII

Here's how we begin. The ego and the id walk into a bar. No one is happy.

Or better. The ego and the id go on a date. Neither of them get what they want.

Or. The ego and the id sit in a cab. The id drunk on art and pumpkin beer and the ego offering to pay, the id saying no this time it is me. And the ego picking up the tab forever after. More than the tab. The id's life of thoughtless impulse feeding from the ego's care and sacrifice. Sucking through a very short straw, then diving in with just teeth and tongue. The id demanding of the ego and not understanding the extent of their demands, so far inside of them. The id in a sling trying to sleep on the floor. The ego, repulsed, looking at the squirming mass about to begin drooling against the hardwood, *Sam — not with your arm — get in the bed please.* The ego asking friends of the id, *is she always like this?* The friends. *Well.*

Well.

The ego standing in the stacks at a bookstore, waiting while the id paces on the phone.

The ego in nothing but boxers and tall socks curled on a too small bed.

The ego in the kitchen with his father, the two of them laughing.

The ego allowing of the id a presumptuous first kiss, the id moving the egos hands down.

The ego making chili, quartering the onion, saving what he does not use.

The ego holding a five week old puppy in his hands. Gentle. *But, where do you bend?*

You would tell me often, *maybe I just can't love that way*. And sometimes when you said it you would cry. And I hated it when you did this. I hated that you could not want me when you were what *I* wanted. And I was cold. I wonder if, or maybe not if but when, I filled you with disgust. I wonder this of you too A.

You are enamored now. You won't tell me if you're falling in love. You are slow and measured and would not share something so important with me, but you are at the very least smitten. And it is hard to watch you feel for someone else — granted someone more deserving, more suiting — the things I wanted you to feel for me.

Deliciously incompatible on every page. Attending to your wants which ran in an infinite parallel line to my own so they would never meet as far down as they walked. But then a few illogical intersections. Our first dinner your visit in Chicago. That night together holding you. And earlier, your virginity. Oh

I laughed at you when you told me you were a virgin, disbelieving. And later, waiting for you wet and desperate as you drove into the city which was barricaded for the Pope's visit. I think of the city then, empty like now, but so hopeful. So different.

When we were young the crush I had on you rivaled the intensity and absurdity of the one I might have for a celebrity. The chasm between us just as impossible to cross. Your music was my favorite, clever and unkind and sharp. And girls would flock around you and close their eyes and sway and sing your lyrics.

Now closer to the ground and solid in the suburbs. Cardigans and a bathrobe. Every morning from your bed watching you engage in the same routine of closet, coffee, shower. Commute. Return. Your contentment on the sofa, not even opening the windows. At peace with what you have built inside.

And you reach out to me. I grab hold too hard.

The id asks the ego for help. The ego weighs all the ways the id is undeserving.

Holding you in Ohio. A soft cry of relief like I was melting. Hardly able to believe I was away. A week of comfort in your apartment, a week when I am not in control. This thawing after the winter of terror in Chicago. I am uprooted and frightened and lashing out. Fighting once over the cost of butter. Which butter? Trying to make a nice meal. The nice butter is better. And you asking me to forgo nice things. Asking me to stop being a hedonist. Stop being lusty or hungry. To, instead of always wanting more, sit with a careful bland portion of existence and be grateful for it the way you are.

Your excesses, your wants, are to be of service. To submit. But in order to accommodate those needs I am the one who must forgo my desires. My rules. I, in providing you with dominance, must be the one who ultimately bows.

Picking me up from outpatient in the dark. Are you worried about me being alone or are you worried I'll be angry I was left alone. You pull. Like offering affection might break you, you pull.

When we are finally over it is long after we should have been over, really we never should have begun at all. I won't come out of the apartment because I am not inside myself. Time nothing. Sitting on the floor. Angry maybe too. And you are waiting, waiting, waiting. When I finally come down and call you, please come back and I am pacing outside smoking cigarettes sitting inside of that summer almost fifteen years before and you return and you say, *I thought there was something wrong with you I thought you were having an episode.* You can't see I am. You can't see how loose my seams are, that I'm barely in my body at all. I am angry you do not know how far away I am, that you do not recognize me enough to know when I am not there. You think I exaggerate every pain even when you are patient with me. To you they are dramatics. I say I want to go to the movies. And you are exhausted after a long week of work. A long night of waiting. The long months of caring for me, fighting with me, waiting. And you say, *I just need to sleep.* And it is over here. Truly over.

I call you A. and you come and sit with me over drinks, closing down the bar, and you listen. It is odd to think we still didn't really know each other. And you say. *It seems like it is for the best, I didn't like the way you two treated each other.*

The id cannot be anything but what it is. The ego too. The id wanting though. The id's impulses creating the emptiness of the bed the id despises.

XLVI

I am informed there is a Craigslist Missed Connection ad that is almost certainly about me. Asking a group of men for cigarettes in my high-rise dark denim shorts. I remember the outfit. I remember my legs in them. I remember breaking the shorts years later at a neighborhood barbecue. Eating and drinking so much not only the button but the zipper bursts. And the pleasure of being rid of the constraint. The white lace top stained with red sauce.

But clean this night and you describe me. Wish you'd smoked. Would like to marry me. Not only is the person who has found this ad certain it is about me, but they are certain they know who wrote it.

We can barely hold a conversation and I believe we only had sex a few times. I remember we got along fine though. Parties. Gardens. The beach. Check, check, check. Quite close. And I spend Thanksgiving with your family. Your mother makes you your favorite muffins in the morning, so happy to have her little boy home.

You sit with me the first time I go to the hospital for a panic attack, thinking it is some other more physical malady. You sit with me the whole night.

LXXXVII

I remember now living in Chicago. As if the storms today have brought the memory with them. I remember I lived in Chicago and so, I remember you. The last time we see one another. You are assigned to my critique panel, you and two older writers I've not worked with. Who are grateful, they say, to have one less thing to read as I've decided to bring paintings. My writing this year is so fragile. I am not insulted by their dismissal of my work, rather, amused by it. And one of them says something deliciously blindly cruel and I make eye contact with you, and it is that same language we'd been cultivating for so long and it broke my heart just this much that we'd been unable to speak it. The next day you leave a big bag of my books at the front desk. Severance.

Every time you used to come to my apartment you would thumb through pages and I'd ask what you were doing and you'd say, *I'm looking for your passport. One of these days I'll find it for you.*

It was lost. I knew it was in a book just not which. When I

finally open the right one. I wish so much I cry that you were there with me to laugh your enormous laugh at my expense.

What is the conversation. Something about love, or the intensity of a youthful crush. I say how can anyone afford to want that much. I'm too tired. And you say, pointedly, *I want that much. Every time.*

A party. You touch my arm or maybe my waist sitting on the couch and I pretend not to notice it. A night of drinks with a playwright in our program and his husband after a reading. Bickering over Sontag. ... *while gay men were dying! And she not even out, writing that essay.* Asking. *Why are lesbians so quiet in their identity?* To me. I smile. I point out women, historically, are primarily possessions. It makes sense their desires would not be interesting enough to come to light. The double meaning that is only for you to understand, none of the men here interested in the complexity or scope of either of our preferences, and the look we exchange. The more red wine I have the more confident I become, the more myself. While you become sweeter, more coy. You tell me I am magnificent after this night. Maybe not this word. But something that strokes my ego in an equivalent way. You are my favorite company. Cornered in an elevator and you offer me old candy from your pocket.

When I find out. I don't ask you about it. You're smarter than me, we both know it. Not only are you smarter but you are more virtuous. More educated in kindness and more generous with others. I'm sure you would have explained it in a way that would make it make sense. I don't tell you why I disappear. I'm sure you will know. Amongst friends it is rumored I am merely jealous — certainly the rumor is not based in untruth.

I meet her once at your birthday party. I am drunk. Of course. It is the period after I've lost the restraining order, where I have a half life. An uncertain future. I am always drunk. You sit on the couch with her and your toes keep knocking together in your socks. As you leave, I am so stupid. I don't even know she is anything more than a friend. But she looks such a child. I say. Is it appropriate to be bringing students to gatherings like this? Our colleague steps in, *I think it depends on the maturity of the student.* I raise my eyebrows. I still don't know what people mean when they say that. A teenager is a teenager no matter how wise or calm or even brilliant they may seem, or be. They are still young. They are not a sexual object for their caretakers to play with.

The same night with the wine. Discussing queer time and the age of consent. *Sixteen is fine, in Europe, amongst men. Certainly no harm there.* Where is the line? I ask. Sixteen? Fourteen? Eleven? When does one stop being a child, and, what if the child is very self-possessed? What if the child is very smart and mature? Where do you draw your lines? Why? I am talking to you. I have shared so much of my life with you. What is appropriate. What is safe?

Of course you are dating her. In all aspects of your life you are so good and correct. A woman besides. Your love must be so enormous, your want so pure, that you are the exception to the rule. And I, ungrateful in rejecting this truth after all the times you held my hand through the storms.

You are in North India and I am in Nepal and that seems like
plenty enough reason to make something work. Your band in
college was one of my favorites. A noisy two piece with a
guitarist and you on the drums. Your long limbs lashing with
unbridled energy and enthusiasm.

We both want to trek in the Himalayas. A photo of you in the
first room we share in Thamel. You are under a string of your
laundry cross legged and smiling. I am proud that my life has let
me be the person to take this photo.

The trek. Happy, our porter, carrying our belongings not
because we are not strong but because this is what we are told to
do and this is what we do. Hiking too far ahead one day and our
guide pulling me back. *It is best you stay with us men.* The tea
houses, many of which I shower in, when I have no right to use
so much water so frivolously.

And they are all dead. The earthquake, mudslides, most of the
population along the Tibetan border killed. We attend a celebra-
tion in a village that I think about sometimes once a week. How

to write it out. I will put it somewhere else, not here — if it is even my place to think on it at all. I wonder though. Are we attending a mass funeral?

I will say just this. A child riding a man's shoulders. Four women linking arms. All the women, thirty or so, dancing in a circle and they pull me in to join them and I have been in the company of only men and I am surprised they recognize me as one of them. I am surprised everyone believes I am one of them.

Riding the bus up to the first base camp and the tires in the mud begin to slip. Sometimes on turns you can feel one or two of them lift up, the thin roads with mountain on one side and drop on the other. And pressed body to body in the bus I see our guide, almost sick with anxiety, and the women on the bus begin to sing together, some crying. And we are both sure this is how we go. You hold my hand so tight.

I fall in love with a soft blanket. I say I would like to give this blanket to my baby if I ever have one. I don't have enough to purchase it for myself — that night I find it wrapped up on my sleeping bag with a little bundle of wildflowers.

This past Christmas. *If you are fine with me having a girlfriend, why not spend a night together in a hotel room in New York?* I turn on you violently. I yell. I am too old to be nothing more than an accessory to others' pain. I am too old to be used this way. I am too tired I will not.

Your face always smiling across the room. Your playfulness with children.

V

A.

At the neighborhood barbecue where I burst my shorts an older photographer, an established artist, asks me to model for him one day. I do, but I think he is too kind to tell me the photos are not what he wanted.

Another dream last night. Sitting with him in a dark corner of my favorite bar in Thamel and he has a suitcase and I have a suitcase. We have nowhere to go, climate refugees, and we decide it is not fair to ask us to stay apart despite the virus still being rampant. The photographer says, *should we fix the photos?* And I say, I am too old. But I am flattered and I oblige. He insists the pronounced muscles in my jaw simply make me fiercer.

I sit in the dark corner holding something to me and as the shutter clicks I begin to cry. I perform my grief. My grief for you A. My grief for all of you. And I shake my head and rend my clothing and the photographer takes photo after photo. When the tears have stopped and I run the back of my rough red hands along my cheeks the photographer looks at the photos. *None of these are usable.*

Nothing here is beautiful.

I say I am sorry. We walk past an uncovered mass grave.

XVIII

I have not read Jane Eyre and this is not a direct address.

I, you — if you can be for gentleness while keeping a safe distance then I think I will use you here for myself — you are sixteen and _____ is a year older than you and she tells you the story of her miscarriage.

Did _____'s body die or the baby's? You know what you should think. You think you know what you should think. But you will never be younger than sixteen again and now sixteen seems nothing like "young," and also you can't imagine being a day over sixteen. Stopping is death. Sleeping is death. Growing is, more pain. More pain like this pain. So who knows what you think. Who knows if you are thinking those days at all.

You will never exist in a time before _____'s story of cupping her hands around the bloody mound of it in the shower. She might say it like it is a joke. She loved it though.

It is her home. Her and her boyfriend's home.

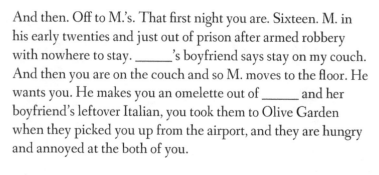

And then. Off to M.'s. That first night you are. Sixteen. M. in his early twenties and just out of prison after armed robbery with nowhere to stay. _____'s boyfriend says stay on my couch. And then you are on the couch and so M. moves to the floor. He wants you. He makes you an omelette out of _____ and her boyfriend's leftover Italian, you took them to Olive Garden when they picked you up from the airport, and they are hungry and annoyed at the both of you.

_____'s boyfriend who draws monsters all day while _____ is in high-school. Or is he in high-school too, or is he older? I'm glad she's away from her parents. His friends visit and when you open your mouth to share your thoughts they mock you for being pseudo-intellectual. You learn this word. A woman must be quoting. You will often doubt everything you say as mere mimicry, hearing in your head this interaction.

Wooden and empty is the home M. finds after he rubs your back and shows you Tarantino. Someone lives on the main floor and the two of you are in the attic, there is one very long very thin staircase straight up to it. Only not you, not really. You're a secret and only allowed out when everyone's away — underage and he's still on probation. The tub is your favorite place to be — it is your home and also your hobby.

If the cops found you — And where will you go, you wonder? Children ask you about the round burns up your legs. No, you tell them. It does not hurt at all.

Making coffee later I can't help but love the sting of the espresso machine. The cauterizing of the wounds on over-washed hands after so long being kept from my favorite pain.

Throughout the quarantine, sitting so close to my space heater there are thinly patterned scars on my calves. The pleasure of the slow scalding, enough to feel without drawing eyes. You are just so tired of being cold though. Cold just as accurate a term as the despised word, _____.

Here it sounds like you are whining. Melodrama.

You haven't decided yet if you can go back. You tried to kill yourself and no one cared. You lived in hell and no one cared. They kicked you out of school for being a drunk, your mother picking you up from the main office in her lunch lady uniform, her pretty mouth, her disgust and horror. You shaved your head and you smoked like a chimney and let boys fuck you wherever they wanted and ___ didn't love you, none of the girls did, *could* — as you are not a man. And whenever you could you snuck out even when there were gunshots. The bed you shared with your sister so cramped — her nightmares her kicking the scratches on your face and arms from her terrors. The pill bottles empty, the laxatives barely doing the work. You just want to breathe. Beating yourself and burning yourself and starving yourself in order to find the room to breathe. The body's pains distracting from the chattering endlessly suffering mind. The mind which invents its own suffering and you don't know what is real and you can't remember what it felt like to rest.

A paragraph here I will not write but that makes me wonder if so many years later the man who kicks in the door, holds up the gun. Maybe you know to be calm because in a way you have met him before.

Theoretically though. Because the reader is wondering. Yes, you, they, can go back.

You are right reader. I am a monster, a whore. I have a vast wealth of sins for which I should be condemned. But reader, can you find a little sympathy for *them*? They are many things and will become worse. But. ...

I cannot even ask. Hold them to the same standards you would anyone else on these pages.

Is your body a home, you wonder? Is M.'s apartment a home? Is it just the tub that's your home? Is every piece of the world your home but for the shared sleeping bag on the hardwood? His sleeping bag. Were you ever home? Can a home be bad or do you make the space bad if you are bad and you call it a home. What kind of structure is your body. ___'s body was a child and her body was the home for a child and now her body is an empty home inside of which a child died. If a home stops being a home, what is it?

If a body is not used for the thing it is made for. What is it?

You are glad the thing is dead though. It seems so much better to be dead.

You don't know yet but one day you'll learn words. Hyper-vigilance. Depersonalization and dissociation. Night terrors. Sleep paralysis. Flashbacks. The way you wake up drenched in sweat.

No furniture. Just ramen. Just two bodies — half in one sweaty bag.

One night you sleep at an old friend's. In your fantasies they let you kiss them when you paint their lips red. You move for the rouge but they tell you not to make them look like a clown. You laugh. In their home you feel like a child and they ask about the cigarette burns on your ankles and they seem foreign but you know tomorrow you will not know where to sleep again.

When you are finished primping you put your friend in a red dress and make them walk through their parent's backyard while you snap photos. They look beautiful but you like taking the paint off too. Like hearing them breathe as they sleep and there are cookies and there are books and everything is so soft.

Then the next night. The cemetery with a bag of Twizzlers and a bottle of gin in your backpack. You remember the graves from your own childhood. You are good and hidden amongst them. The babies make you think of ___. No one finds you. It is the fourth of July. There are fireworks that make you jump. Maybe it is not the full night here.

The night after it is back to the attic. You can never stay away from the single bag, the bath.

M. sees you smoking out front in the morning when he goes to look for work. Maybe he takes the cigarette out of your hands crushing the tip between his fingers but not showing it hurting at all, what a waste. But surely that is a false memory. M. I must tell the reader. Is not trying to hurt them.

It is important for the reader to know that I do not believe M. ever wanted to cause them pain. He proposed marriage to them. He thought he loved them and was showing them love the way he knew how.

This though, verbatim. *You remind me of my mother.* Which is bad. So, you wait by the skate park and find a boy who sent you notes in elementary school. He buys you a large french fries with honey mustard from Wendy's and lets you take a nap in the front seat of his car after you provide him with exhausting affirmations of, yes, you are so cool. The bleachers at the University and the summer nights and the stars. And you cry and cry please don't leave me. And he leaves you. His family will worry.

The next night the attic again. You remind him less of his mother now.

The night after you crawl back to _____'s. They've broken up. She's staying with a friend but her ex is still there. First you drink his rum, then his vodka, then a few of the mixers whose names you don't know. You smoke a full pack of cigarettes on his back patio, one right after the other. But you're too young to buy your own so you save the second pack. Camels. The ex cusses when he finds you drunk and asleep in his apartment and stinking and you blink open your eyes. You can hear him talking on the phone about you. Complaining. He sends M. to collect you. You are so gone you cannot sit up. You remember M. asks before he fucks you and you do not remember you probably assent but you only remember the first thrust from behind on your hands and knees and somehow there is light coming in through the windows and waking up on the floor of an empty room. I can see the room so clearly that I could not give you the picture of it if you took it from me. It is me.

At least now he wants you, right? The first time in missionary, which you offer him, ask from him, but he is too big and it hurts and you could hear children outside and the sound of the children that night too and the open window with the open air are part of you, while he was inside of you on the sleeping bag on the floor. You know it hurt but you can't remember the feeling of it you can only remember the children outside and the warm summer air and after he is finished he stands all six plus and says. *Oh. So this isn't as good as jerking off.*

You still beg your lovers for praise. You just want them to be happy.

At the end of a month, two months, you don't remember — you get on a plane and spend the rest of the summer with your grandmother.

Her cupboard is full of expired soups and her bathroom is full of laxatives even more potent than the ones you left behind. You like the consistency of the soup coming out the way it went in. Like your body is a clean chute for warm liquids and nothing else. Later you will like to watch porn where women gape for this reason. The spotless open hole. You like the idea of the body as one long clean tube, the vagina not even present. All tissue, breasts, muscles, organs, surrounding the tube for mere insulation. Supporting the long clean undulations of enter, exit.

Can this be bad enough, enough to feel this bad?

Why has it written itself so strange.

LXXXVIII

You have the same name as M. Isn't that funny?

We are drinking. I say, I have to go I have to go. You say, *let me follow*. We sit in the first row of *Ms. Julie* and I hold your hand so hard I might break it.

The first time we fuck we are both crying. We are talking about death. Death we've seen, unable to stop the pain the death coming fast and for who knows who next.

Ours are the most vile and hedonistic fucks and you make me all soft. A submissive little slut after years of control and dominance and maleness. For weeks we lock ourselves in my bare walk-in closet. We fuck against the wall and the floor for hours and I am your whore. But I beg you not to tell.

I don't want people to see me. To imagine me *taking* it.

You point out the hypocrisy but do not press.

You are tall with long blonde hair and glasses. A beautiful white man's unearned confidence. You are in a writing degree to explore the shapes of exploding fruit that I still find sensual. I am late to a workshop we are in together and enter the classroom to find you sitting alone at the front of the class, the lights dimmed, and the room bathed in a rust orange light — I am sorry I do not remember your so perfect obsession with the name of the shade — reading a poem aloud about watching a goldfish die on the floor, gasping for breath.

Kicking arousal. I hope I am the dying fish.

We are crying because we have been bad. On the train, I do not remember what we say but we are scolded. We are, too loud.

A.

I see a photo of you A. and it is recent enough and I am, isolated
enough, or maybe just obsessed enough. I wonder often if this is
grief or mere obsession. If I am obsessed with my own grief. As
if I were so lucky to make a choice. As if my masochism ran so
deep. But still, I can feel the skin of your cheeks. You've shaved.
And, maybe I am ill, but I can physically feel you. A little loose
against the jawbone, dry and worn. Stubble still. Lips. It is true
to say, soft … lips. Soft lips. I can *feel* this cheek — on my palm,
on my own cheek, neck, shoulder. I can feel every piece of your
body I was allowed to touch. Your cock inside me, or in my grip,
or against my mouth. Just the shaft brushing my lips as I
worship. Your balls. Your stomach. Your nipples. The dry skin
on your thighs. Your fingers. I dream about your fingers. I wish I
had taken initiative to kiss your feet. Filthy. Taken them in my
hands. Ankles. The bones of your shins. What do your knees
look like? How cruel that I cannot remember your knees. How
much of your body did I waste, assuming I would have time to
assess it later. Had I wept beneath you, bathing you with tears
and cum in want. What could I have done to be allowed some
kind of proximity? No. Closeness. I vomit thinking about you at

odd hours still. Just the absence. Like being punched and I heave whatever is inside me.

And writing here. Remembering again your cheek. I have to leave my desk to stand at my sink and cum. Just remembering the way it felt in my hand. And I weep as I cum. Not the howling sobs of despair I am used to overtaking me but a long quiet weeping of silent tears running down my face relentlessly. And it is a long orgasm so I drop what I am holding and lean my full weight against the sink, waves of release. Water down my thighs. And writing now my whole body shakes still and the tears are on my wrists. And I may have to vomit again.

Last week it was your left ear. So, I am improving.

Everything I've written since I met you has been for your eyes. Even before I am sure I am convinced of you. But when we finally meet. When you thrust it is not just your body but your being. Crashing into me. Crushed by me. When you are near my skin I feel it tugging at my heart and I shiver. We have read this in books, seen this on the stage, but, I get to *feel* it. Know it is not hyperbole but real. It is the first time for me. The first sex where I am truly present. Where you promise, and I trust. I trust you completely to handle me well and I open myself. You are the only person who has touched me.

After a book like this — to discover I had never been touched.

LIX

I am late to see you perform at the Met.

Much later. I tell you the last time we see one another I am writing. I tell you that you, A., have left me. *Another married man? Haven't you done that?* I say I think I am resigned to be the mistress. I say. I don't need anyone to hold my hand. You drink. When you were the age I am now, fixated on your decomposition. You were entering retirement though while I have not yet begun a career. Changing the conversation topic. But I am writing. *Fiction?* No. Sometimes the love of your life leaves you for his pregnant wife and you just have to write memoir for a bit. You laugh.

This conversation in December when you treat me to tickets of your old company's winter show. Wine with the choreographers who do not remember meeting me years and years before at parties. Twenty-one in pink dresses hanging on your elbow. *You must be a dancer?* No, no. Sitting as near you as possible and I would complain I don't belong, and you would always tell me, a little irritated, *you're here. You belong.* This last meeting it is the same. After the wine we are shown to our seats and you are clapped on the shoulders and met with awe and camaraderie like a quarterback on a football team in an old high school film and I am again my old self, an outfit I have bought just for this night, a person of no great value or meaning. The one time I did not feel this way, perhaps New Years day, everyone drunk and smoking. _____, the man you are living with. An ex-politician or CEO, I can never quite remember, but exactly the type you would expect. Grey with a big nose and long ears and reigning from his chair. I draw him in his throne and you smile, hang the sketch on his fridge. Just him, you, me, your choreographer, and _____'s assistant. Always alone in these groups of men. And his assistant after a long day of talking and imbibing, champagne and Chinese food and beer, pulls out a guitar. I kneel in front of him on the floor with my skirts around me singing The Beatles. "Blackbird." "Hey Jude." I remember embarrassing myself often in this apartment. This was not one of those times. I remember it, and I hope I am not rejected in this belief, no, I believe you have confirmed it for me — it was something akin to holy.

The Met too, I was all awe. My first time. My friend, when I finally arrive, pulling a tag off my red dress and fixing something else I've left in disarray. Sighing at me. You are a featured dancer in *Aida* and I have taken a bus up to New York to see you perform. Two tickets. I get my own guest.

After your performance you have a party or are exhausted and my friend and I just want more sound. You kiss me goodbye. A photo of you alone outside the building in first position. The two of us returning though and we stand in the back for *Don Giovanni*. A rich older couple offers us their tickets when they leave at intermission. Something like the fourteenth row on the left hand side of the theatre. And this is my god. Whatever happened in that theatre that night is what I worship. Pure transcendence.

What does seeing you perform make me feel? Something just as intense, if not as loud. If the Met is a hymn in a congregation watching you on stage is like a prayer in a quiet wood. No less spiritual.

The first time I see you dance it is with the first professor. It is the night we get the hotel on Broad and drink wine and hold each other in the bed and see the ballet, his hand on my knee. Transfixed is not even the word. It is not an experience of art I've ever had. I've never seen the body used this way. I've never seen pain this way, love, so clearly expressed. _____, your friend who I still think is the greatest living dancer, does a duet to "Hallelujah." And I cry openly almost as soon as it begins. Her clothing used to bind her, support her. The aching and the trust. She is still dancing, too old, the wrong sized thighs, and working through a litany of injuries you detail for me. She is pure sense though. The form so carefully masquerading behind the feeling. And after this first time I return and return to your shows. Anytime I can.

_____ is wonderful but you are my favorite. There is an anger to your body. You are dignity but you are also ferocity. When I tell my coworkers at the gym, where you are a member, that I am so obsessed — they conspire to see us together. The first date I am like Cinderella and you are dismissive. You have not dated someone normal like me before. A nothing. And when we end you pull this out and throw it at me. When I tell you I have cheated on you and, your rage, a true hot male rage, you lash out at me. *A twenty year old nothing doing this to me.* I tell you this last December, and it has taken almost a decade to be sure of it. I believe I have some value.

But each subsequent date you become more invested. I spend many of my weekends on the bus to New York. Once I remember your urgency, bending me over the bed you have been waiting but I am lonely wanting to kiss. Wandering through the Etruscans at the art museum and dizzy. But also the first time, after seeing you perform, still sweating from the stage and you are living in a large patron's house. That first night climbing up the stairs, there is a large glass shower and I am granted the task of washing the sweat off of you with rose scented soap. Kneeling. This night blurry with luxury and desire and gestures of worship. After I sleep against you in a brass knobbed bed.

You find me funny and strange and introducing me to your world I also find myself strange. At parties. How have I found myself in this room of beauty and money and genius? A simpleton. When out you are prone to excesses, another shot, another bottle of champagne. But sitting alone with you one night on the sofa you have a single milk chocolate stout in front of you. And you say to yourself, *I worked hard. I deserve this.* You say it twice and I confirm before you pour it for yourself. And this is who you are. What you believe. If you work hard then you will get what you deserve for it. But you do not understand the way I do that there sometimes isn't any karmic retribution. Sometimes you work hard and there is nothing, or there is loss, or there is betrayal. And sometimes you do nothing and are rewarded. Often you do harm and are rewarded. And it is harder for you because you want the order, you need the world to be a good world. The deep anger you carry is because it is not. A consumed climate change activist, I remember visiting you at Occupy Wall Street. The pieces you choreograph weaving in your philosophies. And I believe to you it is a personal failure that you cannot yourself be the difference needed to save the world.

We remain close but we never fuck again after my admission. Years later caring for your home while you travel, I only kill half of the plants. We see shows. I do not tell you but I still have your favorite scarf. I do not know why you still want me in your life but I am grateful. I think you might enjoy my company. I think, whatever we had, it was good.

The dance this December. I wanted to show you A., I wanted to explain to you the love I have for it. I want to show you everything I love A.

_____ is the primary dancer despite her broken back, ecstatic and fluid, working through the pain. And how it manages to be a dance about the holidays that is not coy or kitsch but instead a critical exploration of loneliness. So by the end, of course, wet beneath my eyes. You have seen it before leaning forward and swaying with the music, forward in your seat, back, leading the dancers with your hands and _____ isolated in a room, jerking as though with exorcism, drinking and sitting. Jerking. Spinning leaping bounds. With others. Again. Alone. While there are bells. While she is on the stage and you can see love also next to her on the stage. Bells that join together in chaotic single mindedness, utter noise ringing — falling and clattering against the wood of the stage and then tapering off each one. Individual pairs of thighs exiting into the wings. _____. Released of the exor-cism. What color is the light that casts her shadow. Is she so alone there is none.

You are always surprised it makes me feel so much. You see the craft but I am grateful I know nothing of it. Grateful for this place of awed devotion. The belief in something more.

A.

Behind the art museum, the winter suddenly absent the sky turning light and there are families. There are flowers. Drippy with the warm yellow sun in the pillars and you offer to take me inside. *Duchamp? Monet?* But it is too exquisite a day I would be overwhelmed with the beauty.

I ask, am I allowed to kiss you? I have never shown you affection this way in public and I am prepared to be denied the treat. But, you let me. You let me in so close you make the world so easy.

That same museum today covered in a crowd. In banners. *This is not a protest, this is a revolution.* And I scream my assent. And a million pains more enormous than mine scream with me, pressed shoulder to shoulder after the long isolation. Where is the justice? A. you shelter with your wife and child. You say the home is like a boat and the world outside a storm.

A woman touches my arm and I flinch, she offers me water. Yes, I am parched. *This is not a protest, this is a revolution.* Watching the world shift so fast from side to side and you in my heart tilting with it. Such small things, you and I. Like a marble rolling with gravity. Helicopters watching as I walk, as I mourn with the world.

Also, despite myself I am still remembering you. Still grieving you.

I remember after I've forgotten myself. I've run away from you, locked you downstairs while you beg for me to let you up. But even as I resist you do not abandon me. When I return sheepish and I open the door and we are both nothing but pain. Still you hold me again. Still you forgive me and hold me again and you sleep in my bed, and this is the only night I am allowed this luxury.

Waking to your chest.

I say I don't want to touch the flame the flame is hot. I say I am afraid.

You tell me not with you — no reason with you. When I am with you, when I am with you — it is like *this* so what right have I to resent the loss? What right have I to ask for more than the graces I have been given? When they were so good.

Have I emerged? Am I clean? At least I am not afraid anymore. I tell myself I no longer believe in that old world and I fear nothing better and nothing could be worse.

I tell you though, I am so afraid.

Shhhh. You say. *Why?* You say.

With me it is just like finally being warm.

ACKNOWLEDGMENTS

A few of the essays in this book were published previously in —
Communion Arts Journal, A) Glimpse) Of), Anti-Heroin Chic,
What Are Birds, Entropy, and Taco Bell Quarterly. Thank you
for seeing something in them. Entropy's WOVEN Series, a
dedicated safe space for personal stories concerning #MeToo
and sexual violence, published the first essay I wrote for this
collection. WOVEN also published "A Refuge for Jae-in Doe:
Fugues in the Key of English Major" by Seo-Young Chu, which
broke me open. Thank you for that community. And thank you
to M.M. Carrigan and TBQ for including me in something
fucking radical.

Thank you to CLASH for wanting this book. To Christoph
Paul for reading it on an airplane and to Leza Cantoral for such
close attention and confidence. I am so proud to be part of what
you've built. Thank you to Matthew Revert for this gorgeous
cover and Lindsay Lerman for being someone generous and
accessible to look up to during this process.

Thank you to Beth Nugent (who probably hates this book) for
believing in me and being a model human and writer and

teacher. Thank you to Sara Levine for your time and wisdom both in and out of school, your insightful feedback, and all of your support. This book really would not exist without your help. Thank you to all the faculty I worked with at SAIC, both writing and painting, for being real artists who influence for good — and my cohort, who were so ballsy and sweet. Thank you to Andrew Ervin for your consistent support, and for saying it's okay to be scared. Thank you to Michael Kaufmann for your excellent instruction and your patience.

Thank you to **my** students who are brilliant and remind me there is real change coming.

After so many pages I can finally stop begging for your attention A., I know you don't read your ex's books anyways. But for myself, I thank A. for inciting in me this desire to speak. I thank him for the moments, the family mornings especially, long after this book's completion, when I thought I would die of happiness. Mostly I thank A. for leaving me again. So violently. You were right A., it was limiting. You were. And if I'm trying to convince myself I'll leave that here too.

And moving on.

Thank you to Alex Tack and Valerie Saporito, my early readers and my oldest writing friends, and my writing group, Taylor Croteau and Sean Chumley. I would have given up without you all and I can't wait for it to be your turn. Thank you to Bess whose friendship has been a long gift of growing, who asked me to write some version of this book, and who is always my very first reader. Thank you to the friends who kept me alive through the writing of this book, and after. Kurt, Gabby (for pandemic dinners especially), Sean, Kat, Joe, Ewa, Dan, Jesse, Tom, and Arden. For the groceries, the ears, the long afternoons of crying on opposite ends of benches. It is an honor to know the finest people. Whiskey is on me, anytime.

ABOUT THE AUTHOR

Picture by M. Price

Sam Heaps is a genderqueer writer, organizer, and visual artist. They have lived and worked places such as Tokyo, Hanoi, Istanbul, and the North American West. In Hanoi they were a contributing writer and editor at the online arts magazine *& Of Other Things*. Heaps has received support from The Virginia Center for Creative Arts and was a 2022 Tin House Scholar. Heaps currently lives in Philadelphia and teaches writing at the University of the Arts. Proximity is their first book.

WE PUT THE LIT IN LITERARY

clashbooks.com

Troy, NY

EMAIL
clashmediabooks@gmail.com

FOLLOW US

TWITTER

FB

IG

@clashbooks